Eddie Cun

# Clever Car Buying

A step-by-step guide
to buying new
and secondhand cars

Edited by
**Olive Keogh**

Published by ARCLA Research

Published by ARCLA Research
Cloonfad, Foxrock, Dublin 18, Ireland

ISBN 0-9543860-0-0

First edition 2002

©ARCLA Research
Text © Eddie Cunningham 2002.
The moral right of the author has been asserted.

*Printed by*
Standard Printers, Ballybrit Industrial Est, Galway

Design by Phil Murphy

Cover by
Darius Design, Blackrock, Co Dublin

Cartoons by Phelim Connolly

All rights reserved. No part of this publication may be reproduced, stored in a retrieval system, electrical or otherwise, or transmitted in any form or by any means without the prior permission of the publisher.

While every effort has been made to ensure that the information in this publication is accurate, the publisher and author do not accept responsibility for any errors or omissions or for any comment subsequently qualified by a change in the circumstances of a company, or business practice, or legislation.

Neither the author nor publisher accept any liability for any losses or consequential losses incurred by any persons (or vehicles) as a direct, or indirect, result of reading or acting on the advice in this book.

## Foreword

People often feel 'lost' when trying to buy a car. I know that feeling. There are so many cars to choose from and 'unbeatable' offers beckoning, it can be tempting to plump for the first deal that looks reasonable.
But a bad decision can cost you thousands.
Yet a little information can go a long way towards taking the risk out of spending such a large amount of money.
That's what this guide is here for. To offer a sounding board, a referral point.
I hope you can use it as a problem solver, a reference and a step by careful step aid to choosing and buying the right car for you.
If it takes some of the gamble out of buying, it will have served a purpose.
I hope you buy well and drive safely.

*- Eddie Cunningham*

**Bridgestone**

This project is supported by Bridgestone Tyres.
Bridgestone is the world's largest tyre and rubber manufacturer. Founded in Japan in 1931, it currently employs more than 95,000 people in Europe, Asia and America. Its products are sold in more than 150 countries. Its European plants are in Spain, France and Italy.
Bridgestone manufacture tyres for a variety of vehicles - from passenger cars and motorcycles to trucks, earthmovers and aircraft.
Many Japanese and European cars sold in Ireland have been fitted with the company's tyres as original equipment. A host of exotic sports cars, including Ferrari and Porsche are also fitted with Bridgestone's performance tyres as original equipment.
Bridgestone commercial vehicle tyres enjoy a worldwide reputation for superior cost-per-kilometre, while more than 100 airlines use its aircraft tyres.
In 1998, Bridgestone acquired the Firestone and Rubber company, combining the resources of both under one umbrella. This, coupled with an intensive research and development programme, has enabled Bridgestone to remain the world's most technologically advanced tyre company with testing centres in Japan, USA, Mexico and Italy.
Bridgestone tyres are distributed in Ireland by Bridgestone/Firestone Ireland Limited, a subsidiary of the multinational Bridgestone Corporation. A wide range of Bridgestone products are available through the network of First Stop Tyre centres and approved Bridgestone dealers.
For further information contact: 01-8415200.
Websites: www.bridgestone-eu.com
  www.firststop-eu.com

---

*It is the author's intention and the express wish of his family that half the net proceeds of this book go to the National Rehabilitation Hospital to help in the work with, and care for, those injured in accidents.*

## Acknowledgments

This would not have been possible without the help of many friends. I owe them a deep debt of gratitude. Sincere thanks to:

Olive Keogh, Editor, for her unstinting support, extensive research and clinical editing. She re-shaped this entire work and gave selflessly and massively of her time, expertise and talent.

Padraic Deane, Editor Irish Auto Trade Journal, for sharing his extensive knowledge of the Irish motor industry and his persistent, practical and forthright encouragement and help.

Colm Conyngham, Marketing Manager Bridgestone/Firestone Ireland Ltd for his unquestioning support.

Phil Murphy, graphic artist, for his layout design, and his ingenuity in making it possible for me to typeset most of this at home.

John Reilly, Editor Irish Car, for his constructive criticisms, guidance and encouragement.

Brian Jaffray, Declan O'Byrne and Anthony Conlon for their advice and support.

Carmel Foley, Director of Consumer Affairs and Michael Daughen of her Office, for expert guidance; the Department of the Environment for prompt assistance and Brendan Stears, technical expert Toyota Ireland, for helping decipher technical terms.

Irish Independent Editor, Vincent Doyle, and Gavin O'Reilly, Chief Operating Officer Independent News and Media, for their support of motoring over the years.

The many friends and colleagues whose generosity of time and advice made this possible, though they may not have realised it at the time. I will thank them individually.

My brother PJ, who push-started many a banger for me on a wet Offaly morning and is still always 'there' for me.

And 'Pa', who endured many an eventful drive with me.

I owe the greatest debt of all to my family: Maureen, Fiona, Carol, Emily and Laura for their immense support, patience and good company - not least over many thousands of road test miles.

**The Author**   **Eddie Cunningham** is a native of Clara, Co Offaly. In addition to his duties as Night Editor of the Irish Independent, he has been Motoring Correspondent with Ireland's largest daily newspaper for more than a decade. He writes extensively on motoring and motoring related issues.

**The Editor**   **Olive Keogh** is a business journalist who specialises in the motor industry. She is motoring correspondent of Decision magazine, Irish correspondent of Automotive News Europe and contributing editor to Drive! magazine and to Autowoman magazine.

## How to get the best from this guide

This book is designed to be both a quick, incisive guide and an easy reference. With this in mind we have divided it into three sections and mapped it out as follows for your convenience.

**Section 1**

Get in the money-saving frame of mind. Where savings lie and the losses lurk.
**Chapter 1**      **Page 7**

How you can exploit the car chain.
**Chapter 2**      **Page 9**

The resources at your disposal to track down the right deal.
**Chapter 3**      **Page 12**

Turning the 'new' car trap to your advantage.
**Chapter 4**      **Page 17**

Four key phrases that can cost, or save, you time and money.
**Chapter 5**      **Page 21**

Your buying strategy. There is only one. The right one.
**Chapter 6**      **Page 24**

The Cold Call: the clinical way to assess the best deal.
**Chapter 7**      **Page 26**

Buying what you need - the critical points.
**Chapter 8**      **Page 29**

Your fit-and-feel test for any car on the market.
**Chapter 9**      **Page 32**

Buying secondhand - everything you should look out for.
**Chapter 10**      **Page 41**

Buying ex-rentals, UK, Europe - the dos and donts
**Chapter 11**      **Page 50**

The cars, their names and why they might suit you
**Chapter 12**      **Page 55**

Depreciation - great value so long as you know when to buy.
**Chapter 13**   Page 65

Buy/don't buy - no-nonsense verdicts on every model, new and used. An expert guide.
**Chapter 14**   Page 70

## Section II

Paying for it - the financial pitfalls and what you should know.
**Chapter 15**   Page 102

When to hold and when to sell - the implications for your pocket.
**Chapter 16**   Page 107

To test or not to test? The money saving way to find out.
**Chapter 17**   Page 111

**AND JUST BEFORE YOU BUY ...**
The final curtain. A unique ten-point last-minute reality check.
**Chapter 18**   Page 113

## Section III

The trouble cars - getting them sorted. Your rights.
**Chapter 19**   Page 114

Make the test work for you - turn its checklist into your checklist.
**Chapter 20**   Page 119

What those technical terms mean to you, your driving and your car.
**Chapter 21**   Page 126

Read between the lines - what the car ad shorthand reveals.
**Chapter 22**   Page 130

**Appendix**   Page 132
The paperwork involved in buying and selling. *Page 132*
The most comprehensive car checklist available. Designed so you can use it as a 'One-page rating' for any seconhand car you look at.   *Page 136 - 137*

How much it costs to run your car   *Page 138*

**Chapter 1**

# The day you buy

Keep two key considerations in mind when buying any car.
1. How much will it be worth when I come to sell or trade in against another model?
2. How much is it going to cost to run?

**Slippery slope**

Cars lose value, some slowly, some moderately and some at an alarming rate. Putting your money on the right one can save a lot by slowing the rate of depreciation and, consequently, lowering the cost of ownership. That is why the old adage rings so true:
**The day you buy is the day you sell.**
Running costs increase each year. So fuel consumption, service intervals, ease of minor repairs, road tax etc are also major considerations. Never lose sight of these two money burners. (See Page 138 for details of running costs).

**The Depreciation Gap**

It is common for two similar cars, with virtually the same price when new, to lose value at much different rates. You can save (or lose!) €125-a-month, or more, depending on which you buy.

<u>Remember!</u> A buyer on PAYE has to earn nearly €240 a month BEFORE tax to have €125 disposable income. Imagine how we'd feel if our monthly mortgage repayments rose by €125. Yet it is possible to throw its equivalent away on a poor decision.

**Why is there such a difference?**

The rate of the decline in the value of a car involves a number of factors:
The size, type and condition of the vehicle, the make of car, the dealer, the distributor, prevailing marketing conditions such as availability of new cars, secondhands and so on.
But you can never change one thing in the whole equation: the car itself.
How good it is and how well it is regarded by other buyers and the trade itself, ultimately decides how slowly or quickly it will lose value.

## Chapter 2

# The car chain

There are four pivotal points in the car chain: manufacturer, distributor, dealer and you. Knowing how this chain works will help you to make an informed decision about what you buy, when you buy and how much you pay for it.

**Manufacturer**

Carmakers plan years ahead. Even while a new model is being launched, they are working on its mid-life revisions and on its successor. Developing a model to the point of manufacture can cost billions.
Extraordinary to think that, in 10-15 years time, the same car will most likely be squeezed into an oblong piece of recyclable scrap. In between it will be driven many miles, consume thousands of euro worth of fuel, make money for a lot of people, lose virtually its entire original worth and maintain a job-rich service industry. The part that concerns us is how many thousand euro it will cost in running expenses and depreciation while *you* have it.

**Distributors**

In the Republic, there is a distributor for every make of mainstream car. (*See Appendix for list*).
Some are privately owned. Some are wholly-owned subsidiaries of the manufacturer. Some have the franchise for one or more manufacturers.
The distributors sign up dealers to sell their vehicles.
They provide them with backing, support and incentives to reach sales targets.

**Dealers**

Dealers are the backbone of the motor industry.
On their forecourts, you and global car manufacturers meet. Dealers have usually been strategically placed - one for a specific area or region. The system has operated along these lines for generations. But the European Commission plans to alter how cars are distributed and that means this rigid structure is changing. Already new standards of premises and services are compulsory under EU rules with an October 2003 deadline for implementation. And from October 2005, dealers will be free to set up anywhere in the EU. The Commission says the proposals are designed to generate greater competition.

There is also a trend towards a convergence of prices across Europe. In Ireland this is expected to cause a sharp rise in prices unless there is a greater equalisation of taxation across member states – something the EU Commission is anxious to achieve. But regardless of what happens, dealers still need to sell cars and your custom is central to this process.

### Smaller can be better

Larger dealers can benefit from big-volume buying power, specialist salespeople and better after-sales service. But some smaller dealers or garage owners are prepared to fight hard for your business. They often have more time to devote to individual buyers and as a result you may get a better deal. You could also fare better with your trade-in because their overheads are likely to be lower than those of a main dealer.

Always give them a try. We came across an example of this benefitting a buyer in our research. A couple saved €1,900 when trading in a three-year-old Toyota Corolla against a brand new 1.4-litre Ford Focus saloon at a smaller dealer 40 miles from their home after being frostily received by a larger one.

A downside with smaller dealers may be a limited selection of secondhands.

**TIP!** A business that does not show a potential customer the regard they deserve before buying is unlikely to provide it for them afterwards.

### Spare a thought

Good dealers, regardless of size, do not keep you waiting weeks for a replacement part. They have a well-equipped and managed parts department. This becomes more critical as your car gets older. But it is worth checking availability as you move nearer to buying a car in case of initial teething troubles.

### Margins

Despite the glitz and glamour of car showrooms, dealers' profits on new vehicles can be surprisingly small.

Margins can be as little as €200-€300 per car in a competitive market.

Dealers make their money on the sell-on profits of trade-ins, servicing new cars bought from them and selling (often costly) spare parts.

Margins on used cars surge and dip. They plunged during the glut of 2001 when demand was slack. Dealers got burned in the 2000 rush and swung from quoting generously to ultra conservatively for trade-ins.

Those who fared best, in what was often a bloodbath for dealer and motorist alike were buyers who had no trade-ins and owners of well-regarded marques.

But everyone trading in against a new (or newer) car at this time got less for their own vehicle and it cost them more to change.

A few years earlier, good used cars were like gold dust and the cost of change was proportionately lower.

The moral of the story is that timing can be critical so it pays to follow trends and shop around if you are planning to buy or sell.

**TIP!** You can save up to €1,500 (and sometimes more) by shopping around.

Chapter 3

# The information roundabout

Obviously the more you keep in touch with what is going on, the better chance you have of anticipating, recognising and getting a good deal.
Car manufacturers never rest. They always have a new model, or a revised version of an existing one, on the horizon. If they slacken, a competitor will capitalise.

**New arrival**

Before you buy, make sure your dream car is not about to be replaced by a brand new model.
The arrival of a new 'baby' can devalue its older sibling by a substantial amount in a short period of time.
So always check before you commit yourself.
Some sales people can be vague about when a new or revised version is due.

**TIP!** Always make a point of asking when the next 'new' version is coming. If you don't get a perfectly straight answer, suspect there is something afoot.

**Private eye**

This is where you can begin to get that 'lost' feeling.
But it is easily countered.
You certainly do not have to rely on the salesperson for clues.
With a little effort you can quickly and independently learn a lot.
Here's how:
Over a few weeks, browse the motoring columns in your daily or weekly read to get an easy, quick 'fix' on imminent new arrivals, and what is coming over the next six to twelve months.
This is a fast, low-cost way of getting such pertinent information.
For real immediacy check in with one or two of the main consumer motoring motoring websites. (See Appendix)

**Up to speed**

Most newspapers, motoring and general magazines also produce a number of car supplements during the year.
Those appearing between October and March usually give a short assessment of every new car on the market. Virtually all carry updates on what is due over the subsequent six to twelve months on a manufacturer-by-manufacturer basis. And they publish up-to-the-minute prices on every car on the market. That means you can quickly get up to speed.

**TIP!** Keep the price lists and motoring specials for reference. Use the weekly updates to flesh out your knowledge and focus on the cars that might suit you.

**What to look for**

Here's an example of what you can find in one of those columns:
*'A new XX is coming in three months time. It will have a choice of three petrol engines (1.4, 1.6 and 1.8) and two diesels (1.9 and 2.5), high levels of standard equipment and will be bigger, roomier and more economical than the current one.'*

And you were going to buy its outdated predecessor as 'new'!
Even if you still decide to, you now know the full circumstances of your purchase. And you can turn that to your advantage by bargaining for a better deal on the 'old' one.
Knowledge is hard currency in this business.

Maybe an updated, rather than brand new, model is due.
So you might read:
*'XX are bringing in a revamped version of their YY. And there will be a booted version in the line-up for the first time. Additional equipment includes side airbags, CD player, new upholstery, electric windows and mirrors.'*

This may suit you much better than the model you were thinking of buying - for several reasons.

Firstly - the updated version is likely to be worth more for longer, be better equipped and have more safety features.

Secondly - even though it may cost more, the additional safety and/or comfort items being offered as standard can add up to more than the price difference between this and the older one. That is particularly true if you were to pay for the additional items individually.

Thirdly - in some cases there may be no price rise if the distributors are anxious to gain market share.

### On the spot

However, if you decide to buy the current model, use knowledge of the new one's imminent arrival as leverage.

Put the dealer on the spot. Say you'll wait for the new one, or a new one from a competitor, unless you get a better deal on the outgoing (often called 'runout') version. Bargain to gain a good cash discount or its equivalent in extras such as a sunroof, metallic paint. You have nothing to lose by trying.

### Ad-ding to your knowledge

Car advertisements*  in the print media also provide a rich, if obvious, source of information on new and secondhand vehicles as they often carry extensive price and equipment levels for individual models.

**Tip!** Use the price quotes in the ads to deduce which secondhand cars are holding most value. And, by extension which make most financial sense to buy new.

This is not an exact science but can give good clues to how the market views different models.

If you have a new-car price list from one of the motoring specials you can fairly quickly see, from the secondhand prices now being quoted, how some cars lose value more quickly.

Don't be surprised to see some have lost as much as 55-75% of their value in three years. Of course new-car prices three years ago would not have been as high, but they are unlikely to have risen by such a significant amount to affect the overall picture.

Depreciation is an expensive business. That's why the emphasis here is on buying the one with the long term pedigree.

The price comparison, however unscientific, is a good way to begin deciding what might suit your motoring needs and make financial sense in terms of holding value.

*An explanation of the main abbreviations used in car ads is provided in Chapter 22.

**Using the net**

Some motoring websites have plenty of information about new cars. And some have links to distributors' and dealers' websites which will speed up your car search process.

A number of Irish distributors also have websites which are linked to their dealerships. You can learn a lot about individual cars this way.

A number of distributors' sites allow you to 'build' your own car on-line. Add whatever equipment you want to the basic car, and then click a button to find the cost of 'your' motor before going near a garage or dealer. It's a real time saver, though of course it is still a MUST to physically 'fit and feel' any car you're thinking of buying.

**Well worth it**

Do not be put off by what can appear to be a car maze. You can learn a lot by glancing through the ads, or motoring editorial while you have a paper or magazine in your hands.

TIP! Keep the price lists from the paper or magazine. They provide outline details of engine size, model variations and allow close price comparisons between marques.
They can also help you draw up a shortlist.

**The brochure beat**

Pick up a few brochures from the dealers in your area. They have good detail and may give you a better feel for the cars as they let you compare specification levels between the models. Brochures are useful to have when you come to phone/call on the dealers about prices. We deal with that in Chapter 7.

**Get some Satisfaction**

Another way of zoning in on the cars that come within your scope is to look out for published reports of how satisfied owners are with their vehicles. Several 'satisfaction surveys' are published each year. The best known are the JD Power surveys which have covered the US, Britain and now Germany.

Another is the BBC Top Gear survey. Most of the cars in this are, or have been, on sale here. The one published in September 2002 canvassed more than 37,000 owners of 120 models from 33 manufacturers of cars from 1997 to 2001.

Another good indicator is the Which Car? survey.
Details of such findings are widely reported in the media.
Use them to add to your knowledge pool. As they deal with older as well as relatively new cars, they are relevant for buyers of new and secondhand vehicles.

But remember they are a useful research tool, not a car buying bible, as more recent models may have been substantially improved.

## Chapter 4

# Avoiding the 'new' car trap

New models are developed and marketed more quickly these days. The average new-car-to-new-car interval is now six-to-seven years

**Cycle of change**

You can roughly divide up its cycle like this:
**1.** For the first two years a brand new car is left largely untouched as sales build up.

**2.** During year three or four, the vehicle will be revised to maintain sales. There may be small changes to the styling. New engine options and bodystyles may be introduced at this time as well.

**3.** As the countdown to the new-new model begins 'special editions' with extra equipment at no extra cost, are often rolled out. And there may be further small cosmetic changes such as new light clusters to freshen up the car's looks.

So the 'same' car changes quite a bit over its lifetime. And the values of preceding versions almost invariably dip when a newer one arrives. Hence the need to be absolutely clear on what 'new' means.

## What's new pussycat?

In car speak, 'new' covers a multitude.

It can mean a totally new model with a totally new name. It can mean a totally new version of an old model in that it retains the same name but is technically brand new and looks substantially different.

Or it can mean a revised version of an existing model - but the manufacturers describe it as new.

It can be difficult sometimes to distinguish between the real 'new' and the promotional 'new'.

Especially in a business where everything is 'new'. Have you ever heard a dealer describe a car as old except when describing your trade-in?

What follows is designed to help you differentiate between the new-born motor and the pensioner in teenage garb.

Knowing the difference can tip the buying scales in your favour and save you a substantial amount of money.

### New, used, revised and revamped

### New-New

A car is new when it completely outstrips the previous one in virtually all departments: shape/design, mechanicals, interior, equipment etc. We'll call it new-new.

### Revamped/revised

These are current models given a mid-life makeover by the manufacturer, usually within three-to-four years of their arrival. But they are NOT new.

A revamp may amount to no more than a fine tuning of the suspension, redesigned light clusters, spruced up interior, new dashboard or more equipment. Or it may embrace a radical overhaul of many departments.

Manufacturers often add new components that will be in the next brand new car.

Such revamps can, in the heat of enthusiastic advertising hyperbole, be described as the 'all-new XX'.

But they are not.

Price rises usually coincide with such upgrades.

The critical factor is to show you know it is not 'new-new'. You are well positioned to profit by bargaining hard on that basis.

### Revamped/revised again (and again)

Describing subsequent revamped/revised cars as 'all-new' is stretching credulity, but it has been done.

Such junctures in a car's lifecycle usually amount to no more than window dressing as its successor is likely to be waiting in the wings.

This doesn't mean you should pass on the current model. But if you do purchase, at least you know the circumstances and should use the full implications of the new car's imminent arrival to get a better deal.

**TIP!** Find out exactly how 'new' a car is before making any decision. Use knowledge of new car arrival to drive a better bargain on the outgoing model.

**The birth and delivery of a new-new car**

Like a Hollywood blockbuster, a new car needs the oxygen of publicity. Initially, there is the report/rumour/announcement that XX is bringing out a brand new model next year.

**First gear**

This starts the time-and-value clock ticking on the existing one. Some distributors want as much as possible known about the new one. Others are reluctant to say anything that would hinder sales of existing stock.

**Second**

The official unveiling of the new model often takes place at a major motor show. The amount of detail given can vary from skimpy to extensive. Either way the motoring press will carry information and you will be aware of what's coming if you browse the motoring sections.

**Third gear**

Manufacturers usually hold an international launch for initial on-the-road sampling of the new car. Motoring journalists (your representatives) are invited to attend briefings and to drive the new model.

**Fourth**

They report their findings and opinions in their columns.

**Top gear:**
**It's here**

Shortly before, or when, the new car arrives in Ireland, the prices, engine line-up and specification packages are announced.
And test drive reports begin to appear in the press. These should give you a feel for how the model performs on Irish roads. The acid test is how price, space, equipment, economy, handling, visibility etc compare with rival cars.

**Making the time lag pay**

Clearing the way for a new model can be a tricky business for the dealer but a bonus for you.
To smooth an old model's passage, the manufacturer usually adds extra standard equipment (CD player, leather upholstery, special alloy wheels).
Your knowledge of an imminent new-new arrival can save you hundreds of euros if you shop around because some dealers may have more old stock than others.

**Special deals**

Carmakers with pressing targets can also introduce special deals on specification, price or finance to boost sales of a particular model or range.

**TIP!** Save money by checking with a few dealerships in your general area. Even if best value is found in the furthermost dealer, you can use the information to reduce prices nearer home.

However, perfectly legitimate offers can sometimes mean better business for the dealer than you.
Whatever the offer, try to boil it down to two essentials.
**1.** How much is the car really costing without any of these promotional frills?
**2.** How much is it really costing with them?
Do your sums and take your time.
Do not be overly swayed by 'Offers Must End' promotions.
There are always more offers, always more cars and always more special editions and deals.
Here's how doing your sums can save you money. Say you bought in February when the list price (fully explained in Chapter 5) was €14,000 and you got a moderate 5% (€700) discount.
Come May and they're offering free road tax, worth €500, for two/three years with the same car. You're on a winner surely?
Yes, if you still get the discount.
No, if you don't. Here's why: If you have to pay the full list price to avail of the deal the car is costing €700 more than in February. Despite €500 worth of road tax under the special deal, you are €200 worse off. You may still decide it's worth doing - if for no other reason than it is a few months younger - but it is not the money saving deal it claims to be.

**Chapter 5**

# Four key terms that can cost you money

When buying a car there are four phrases with serious implications for your pocket.

**1. Full list price**

This is the total quoted price including all taxes and added charges, such as delivery from the importation compound to the dealer, pre-delivery inspection (PDI), cleaning and number plates. The list price is usually open to negotiation, as we'll see.

**2. Ex-work price**

This price does NOT include delivery and related charges. Ex-works is the tax inclusive price of the car as it sits on the dockside. It is the figure usually given for the majority of cars on price lists and in the motoring press. But there will be an absolute minimum €240 added for delivery to the dealer, for number plates and other related charges. Some dealerships charge €500, and more, depending on the marque. These charges make the difference between ex-works and full list price.

**3. On-the-road/cash straight deal price**

Effectively this is what you end up paying for the car. It is the price you and the dealer reach at the end of all the negotiating. Its final amount can be determined by so many factors - such as scarcity of the new car, demand for your secondhand if you have a trade-in, sales targets, profit margin policy, time of year (dealers anxious to meet targets in the autumn/early winter may give higher discounts) and so on.

Before the big boom in car sales in 2000, a 7% -10% discount on the full list price was widely applied - virtually always on a cash or straight-deal transaction. This contracted to no discount at all at the height of the 00-reg demand.

Generally speaking, it can vary between 3%-10%. However, the system can cause uncertainties where there is a trade-in. That's because it can be difficult to distinguish between what you are getting for your old car and what you are really paying for the new one. In Chapter 7 we have a way of clearly establishing both values and making the list system work for, not against you.

Fiat and Alfa Romeo operate the transparent on-the-road Open Book system, which means the price includes all charges, at all their garages. They do not concern themselves with list or ex-works prices.

### 4. VAT and VRT

The price of your car includes two major Government taxes:
(i) VAT and (ii) Vehicle Registration Tax (VRT)

### (i) VAT

The distributors agree the price of a new car with the manufacturers. This is called the pre-tax price. VAT at the prevailing rate is levied on this. VRT is then calculated by a complex process and added. It therefore becomes a tax on a tax.

### (ii) VRT

Vehicle Registration Tax was invented by the Government to replace excise duties on cars when frontier free Europe dawned in 1993. The Government told the EU it could not sustain the massive annual loss of revenue from excise and other motor-related duties. But the EU Commission wants such systems replaced by more equitable environmental and usage-based taxes. It may be some time before that happens.

### How it is calculated

The amount of VRT payable is based on the expected retail price of a new car, not on its pre-tax price. This is known as the Open Market Selling Price (OMSP) which includes taxes etc.

VRT* is calculated at 22.5% of this selling price on cars with engines up to, and including, 1400cc.

It comes to 25% on the price of cars with engines from 1401cc to 2000cc. And is levied at 30% on the OMSP of cars over 2000cc.

Taxes, but especially VRT, add thousands to the pre-tax price of a car. *(\*As of October 2002)*

**Check engine size**

Because of the different VRT rates, please check on the real size of the engine in any new car you are thinking of buying at home. If importing, be aware of it for new and used (See Chapter 11). Terms such as '1.4-litre' are bandied about loosely.

A car with a 1370cc engine may be called a 1.4-litre. It attracts VRT at 22.5%.

Yet a 1.4-litre with a 1401cc engine is hit for 25% because it is in the next taxation category. Being aware can mean a tidy saving.

**TIP!** Check the *exact* cubic capacity of an engine and save money.

## Chapter 6

# Your buying strategy

Much of what follows applies when buying a new or used vehicle.

**Buy them both**

Buying from a good dealer or garage is vital. Dealers in general have acquired an undeserved bad name. A few deserve it. Most do not and are high-calibre business people offering a professional service. They depend on your business and repeat custom.

<u>TIP!</u> When you buy the car you should also 'buy' the dealer.

**Cost of Change**

The financial side of car buying can get complicated if you let it. But it does not have to. Of utmost importance to you is how much it will cost you to buy the new(er) car - in other words the Cost of Change.

Any new-car deal you do will involve the discount (or lack of it) off the list price and the changeable value of the trade-in if you have one. You are looking for just one thing. How much is it going to cost to change?

The same applies if you are buying secondhand.

All other factors being equal ask yourself which deal costs the least?

**Robbing Peter Paying Paul**

A dealer can increase his quote for your trade-in on foot of a better offer to you from elsewhere.

How is that financially possible?

Obviously he can take a smaller margin.

But he can also rob a little from Peter to pay a little to Paul. Here's how: Instead of giving you a few hundred euro discount on the new car, he can now stick rigidly to the list price and add the few hundred euro to the valuation of your trade-in.

Effectively both new-car and trade-in vehicle valuations have increased.

But you can end up paying the same amount to change cars. The motor industry knows that an increased valuation of a person's trade-in can swing a deal - even though a buyer is not really gaining anything. It appears we all like to think we're getting a good price for 'our' car. The best advice is to stick to one figure only - the real Cost of Change.

**Your lucky day**

Knowing about other reasons for variations in trade-in quotes can help pinpoint your best outlet and save money.

**1.** Dealers have different customer profiles. Your trade-in might suit one because they currently have demand for such models.

A dealer can give a better price in the expectation of a quick re-sale.

If you don't shop around, you will not fully pick up on, and benefit from, these marketplace shifts.

With a different car on a different day, another dealer might offer a better deal.

In a check of nearly 30 dealers - all selling the same marque - we found several four-figure differences between the least and most expensive where we were 'trading in' against a new car.

**2.** Prices can also be influenced by pressure to reach sales targets, lower overheads, a strategic decision to settle for lower margins and so on. And, of course, a good salesman will always get more for his dealer than a poor one.

3. Price is influenced too by a dealer's reckoning of the costs involved in repairing the trade-in before selling it on.

And he must calculate on taking trade-ins on subsequent sales plus the cost of guarantees for them.

Effectively he has to 'buy' another car of diminished value each time and, in most cases, sell on with greater difficulty. That can sometimes mean having to wait a long time to make real profit. That's why they tend to err on the side of caution - to the buyer's detriment.

Alternatively, he may have your car destined for a trade buyer, or auction, which means he has to 'buy' it from you at a good price.

It is important to be aware of this if you are trading-in a model that a dealer has in plentiful supply - or if their compound is full of cars.

On the other hand, if you are buying secondhand a dealer with a long list of used cars tying up capital will very often listen to a reasonable offer - even if it means making little or nothing on the transaction.

**Chapter 7**

# The cold call strategy

This plan is designed to get the clearest idea of the gap between the *real* selling price of the new car and the value of yours.
Let's call this the **Ideal** or **Minimum Cost of Change**.
It means you have a solid price basis on which to calculate, compare and bargain.

**Straight quote**

Telephone 'cold' calling will save you a lot of time and effort when shopping around for a new, or used, vehicle.
Your 'first call' objective is simple. You want a straight deal/cash price quote. This will quickly show which dealers are interested in giving discounts and those who are not.
It means you can eliminate the more expensive ones.
And you can save the better quotes until later. At that stage you will be calling to try out the car and conduct more proctracted negotiations with your shortlist of dealers.
If you are trading in or buying seconhand, you should visit the best-price dealers to see the car(s) you are being quoted for - and for them to see your trade in.

**Quote/unquote**

Here is the first-check routine.
*Call the dealers/garages you believe to be most suitable in terms of their selection, make, model, reputation and proximity.
* Make it clear it is your initial trawl through a number of dealers.

*Impress upon them that you are genuinely shopping around. Dealers may be reluctant to give you their best price if they suspect a competitor garage is making a check call. Tell them you are using this phone-around to cut down your shopping list and it's in their interest to give you their best quote. They may still be reluctant. So if they ask you to drop in, it may be worth your while to do so.

*Assuming you can still talk business on the phone, be as specific as you can about the make(s), model(s), engine size(s) and bodystyle (saloon, hatchback, estate etc) you are interested in.

*You want to know what Car XX or YY will cost on a straight deal.

*Before finishing, re-confirm the version(s) and major items of standard equipment on each.

 *Repeat the routine with other dealerships on your list.

**Good steer**

These quotes will give an excellent idea of where the best *cash price/straight deal* lies, especially if you don't have a trade in.
If you have a car to dispose of, you could sell it privately and take the best of the straight deal offers. It is the ideal situation. But many find it time consuming and awkward. So it is more likely you will trade-in your current car to part-finance the deal.
And that means visiting the best price dealers.

**How much?**

At the dealership, ask the salesperson how much it will cost to buy Car XX with your own as a trade-in against it.
Now you can quickly establish the real value of your car to the dealer as you already have his straight deal selling price for the new(er) one.
Without being in any way confrontational, make the salesperson aware that you know their straight deal selling price of the new(er) car and bargain as best you can on that basis.
Save this trump card until you reach what you believe to be close to the dealer's best price.
Then take time out to think about it. Repeat this exercise at a few other dealerships. You will then be well equipped to make your final comparisons, and ultimate decision, on where to buy.

**Good sample**

You should try to get Ideal or Minimum Cost of Change prices for identical same car(s) from at least two, preferably three dealerships. It saves money, time and travel.
Other factors, such as which car physically suits you best, equipment levels, distance from dealer, how they treated you, their reputation for after-sales service etc, must be considered.

**Good for used**          But being clear on price paves the way for such considerations and we will deal with them later.

**Good for used**          The complicating factor with secondhands is the variable condition of the cars on the market. But this exercise can help eliminate the more expensive dealers at any given time and provide a focused shortlist.

**Lower quote**           When you come to physically try out the cars, especially new vehicles, the critical factor of specification comes into play if prices between different makes and models are close. We'll deal with that in Chapter 9.

**Chapter 8**

# Buying what you need

There is no point in making the right financial decision if you don't buy the right car.

**Fitting in**

Buy what you need to meet your practical and lifestyle requirements in the medium term. In other words, don't buy a two-door coupe if you need a car to take three children to school every morning. Make the wrong decision and you may have to live with its physical and economic shortcomings for a long time.

**Plan your next move**

When you are drawing up your shortlist, try to consider your requirements over the next two to three years. Are they likely to be markedly different from what they are now? Will a newer version of your current model, for example, accommodate your requirements? Or should you go for a larger executive, a smaller hatchback, a roomier family car?

Your circumstances may be changing but it is easy not to have fully thought out their implications when you come to buy.

You may need a car for a growing family, or room for a wheelchair, two dogs, elderly passengers etc.

Making the right buy this time will save you money.

**Outgrown**

It is better to choose a car children will grow into rather than out of. Otherwise you could be facing two changes of car within a short time.

That would involve two outlays instead of one. It is also most likely you will take a hit on the reduced valuation of your first buy. A car costing €14,000 eight months ago could now be worth as little as €11,000. And the larger one you should have bought could be €500 more expensive.

**The switch hitch**

Reasons for changing cars can vary from the practical to the personal. Perhaps you just feel like a complete change from a boring old saloon to something snazzy and powerful.

But remember that switching between car types can hurt financially. Apply the cost of change criteria before you jump.

Some dealers may not have as good an outlet for your old model. So test the water by pinning down the cost of changing. If it varies widely between three or four dealers, garages or secondhand outlets then the one with the lowest Cost of Change quote probably has more, and better, outlets. This is important as potentially substantial sums of money are involved.

**Downsizing**

Trading down also has its pitfalls. Buying a smaller car, now the children have gone, may seem like a good idea but trading in a three-year-old 2.5-litre petrol executive saloon and buying a new 1.6-litre five-door hatchback is not the greatest match for a good deal. You may save more by selling your car privately/separately and buying 'straight'.

On the other hand it may make more financial sense to hold onto your existing car for another year or two. By doing so, it loses more value but its reduced selling price may tempt a broader spectrum of potential buyers.

**Hop, skip and jump**

One approach is to downsize gradually.

If you are in a mid-size executive vehicle, try trading it in against a car from a segment below such as a compact executive (details of different car sectors: Chapter 12). Try to stay with the same marque as you are more likely to get a better deal.

Next time round you can trade down another niche if you wish. At this stage you will also find it easier and less financially risky to switch marques. Avoid trying to jump too many segments at once. It can mean the years spent working up to, and maintaining, a larger car are frittered away in one deal.

**TIP!** Use your next car change to think about what you will need in two/three years' time. Should you be moving in that direction now to lessen the subsequent cost?

**Don't break the bank**   While circumstances may force you to buy a more expensive car, try to stay well within your means, even if it involves buying an entry level model.
Do not over-stretch.
Each extra €1,000 borrowed can generate €300 in interest charges for a three-year period.

## Chapter 9

# Buying new: your fit-and-feel test

Now it's time for a reality check - to see if the best-value cars you have pinpointed as possible buys 'fit' you and your requirements. It will also give you an opportunity to see how the dealerships on your list measure up.

The following two-step routine is designed to provide an easy way of finding the cars that suit you best. The emphasis is on new cars, but the advice applies in large measure to used vehicles too. You can use it before, during and/or after you've sampled the cars. Indeed, using it afterwards (but before you close the deal of course) can help spark memories or recollections of items you may have forgotten.

**Getting a taste for it**

It is a good idea to have some brochures so you can peruse their details at your leisure before trying out the cars for size.
It also means you can ask any questions that may arise from them when you arrive to see if the car 'fits' you.
Always make sure you clarify what is standard equipment and specification across the range.
Then take plenty of time to try out the car for size - you will have to live with whatever you buy for a long time.

**The Great Sit-in**

Use this initial checklist for each car you try out.

**Comfortable?**

Am I comfortable in the driver's seat? This applies to everyone but particularly anyone with a history of back pain, short reach or stiffness. Comfortable means the seat adjusting for you, not you for it.

**Well adjusted?**

Does the seat and/or steering wheel adjust sufficiently to give more leeway to change the driving position?
The longer you are sitting in the car, the more your body 'settles'. Therefore you may need to raise/lower the seat and adjust the height or reach of the steering wheel (how near or far it is from you?). If you can't alter the seat or steering wheel positions or

they won't adjust any further, you will notice the strain in everyday driving. Also remember that others may be driving your car and may need to be consulted. Make sure the seats support your back and thighs. Sitting for only a minute or two can give you a false impression. Take your time. The seat must fit. Many cars now provide lumbar support adjustments for the driver. Check.

**Seatbelt?** How does the seatbelt feel? Are others, likely to be driving the car, comfortable with it? Seatbelt comfort can be a real problem for women. Unless the belt is extensively adjustable it may cut into their breasts. Lack of adjustment can also be a problem for tall drivers whose comfort can be seriously compromised by an overly restrictive belt. And if they can adjust the seat (usually backwards) how much room will it leave rear seat passengers? Where two people will be driving the same car frequently, both should spend time with it.

**Out of reach?** How easy is it to find and reach major instruments and switches/controls? Do you have to stretch uncomfortably to reach the radio dials, or change the ventilation settings?
Do you have to deflect your vision from straight ahead to do so? If so, this may not be the car for you.

**Near or far?** How easy is it to reach the accelerator, clutch, brakes, handbrake and gear stick? If have to shift your body weight a lot to reach the clutch, for example, this car doesn't 'fit' you.
Some cars have central consoles that make it awkward to operate the handbrake. Check this is not the case with the car you are looking at.
If you are not very tall, you may have to sit quite far forward. This is likely to place the handbrake well behind you and put a strain on your arm and shoulder as you reach back to use it.

**Access** How about getting in and out? Some cars pose a nightmare for people of above-average size or height, or those with restricted movement. If you have someone with limited mobility as a regular passenger, check out the seat height. Also check the roof height to see how low they have to bend to get in.

**Wide open rear doors?** This is important for young and old who need easy access.

| | |
|---|---|
| **The children?** | Settle the driver's seat to accommodate yourself. Then sit directly behind it and assess the space there. This is a good indication of the room backseat passengers will have when you are driving. Individual seats in the back (such as those available in many MPVs) are ideal for children as they avoid 'space' wars.<br>Check if there are child locks on the rear doors. Is there a facility to which a child seat(s) can safely be attached? And what sort of upholstery is used? Is it hard wearing and unlikely to show up dirt and scratches?<br>If you have pets these questions are important too. |
| **What about the boot?** | Will the boot/luggage area take the big once-a-week shop, the three (or four) golf bags etc? Is it easy to open and close the tailgate/bootlid? |
| **The engine size?** | Mentally run through a normal day and think of the demands on an engine. Then think what you do in your leisure time. Do you need an engine capable of towing a boat, caravan or small trailer without struggling? You should buy as small an engine as you think you will realistically need for everyday purposes.<br>Don't pay extra for more power if you don't really need it. |
| **Will it fit?** | Sounds obvious but check first. If you are planning to park in your driveway or to garage your car, make sure it fits before you buy. |
| **Safety first** | While giving the seat the 'five-minute test', pay particular attention to the details on safety in the brochure.<br>Check how many airbags are standard and if the car has anti-lock brakes, a fuel cut-off system etc (See Chapter 21 for an explanation of technical terms). |
| **Knees up** | While sitting in the car, run your hand around the contours of the lower dashboard. Are there sharp corners and/or objects around your shins and knees? Do you feel constrained or restrained by bulky armrests on the doors or protrusions from the lower dash? How comfortable, cramped, secure do you feel? |
| **Belt up** | Are there three full seatbelts in the rear or is there only a lap-belt for the centre passenger? Regardless of passengers' age and size, you should try to ensure there are three full belts. The passenger in the middle is extremely vulnerable in an accident. |

**Safety**

Other items to consider (brochure details may help) are:
How well is the front of the car designed to 'crumple' in a head-on crash? What systems are fitted to minimise injury i.e. does the brake pedal 'deform' on impact to avoid injuries to your legs in an accident? These are important considerations.

**Look and see**

Check the car's all-round visibility. Do you feel happy and comfortable with the amount you can see out of the corner of your eyes in the rear view mirrors and in the wing mirrors?
Some cars have large broad pillars which can make it difficult to see and create a 'blind spot'.
Some cars also have rear vision reduced back seat headrests. You should be able to see easily to the front, rear and laterally without having to strain. Don't compromise on this.

**Air and heat**

If you can, check the fan for speed, power and effectiveness. Turn it on to see how quickly you feel its effects. A ventilation system that cannot quickly clear a misted windscreen or cool the cabin is a nuisance and a possible danger. You may try this to far greater effect if you take a test drive. Air conditioning is fast becoming a popular addition to the specification on Irish cars. The more you pay the better the system. These can be manually or electronically controlled. More expensive cars generally have a refined form of air conditioning called climate control.

**Lights**

If you are likely to have a car full of passengers or to tow a trailer/caravan regularly you should make sure there's a headlamp height adjuster so the beams can be lowered to avoid dazzling oncoming drivers. Ideally there should be a 'lights on' warning tone to remind you to switch off and avoid a flat battery.

**Boot it**

Take time to check the boot. Imagine yourself lifting the shopping, or a child's buggy, or a wheelchair over a high rear 'lip' on a wet, windy day. A low-loading sill with a good broad 'mouth' to the boot area is the ideal. Also check to see how easily the rear seats fold to provide further luggage space.

**Getting the door**

See how quickly the door opens outwards. If it is too lightly sprung, it could easily damage another vehicle in a car park, or scrape against a wall, or be wrenched by high winds. If it's too stiffly sprung, you run the risk of it closing on your shins just as you're getting out - especially on an incline.

**Handbags at two paces**  Modern cars offer little more than matchbox accommodation for purses or handbags as the old glovebox space now usually accommodates the passenger airbag. Look for a good 'pocket' on the inside of each front door, storage points under the dash, a safe place to keep a few coins (for tolls and parking) and somewhere convenient to hold a soft drink can or tea/coffee cup.

**Poor reception**  Make sure you can get good radio reception on the channels you want. There is a big variation in the quality of reception.
If, and when, you take a car on a test drive, stop somewhere safely, and run through the stations on Medium Wave and FM. Drive a little with the radio on. Poor reception shows up more quickly that way and you can check for any buzzing and interference caused by the engine.

**Equipment**  Brochures provide a good basis for comparing equipment levels on different models and marques.
Depending on how anxious a manufacturer is to sell a particular model, there may be a big difference between similarly priced cars as we've seen.
Equipment levels are improving all the time and, in real terms, mean cars are better value.
But make sure you are paying for what you want. There is no point in having costly, unnecessary additions.
For example, you are unlikely to need cruise control. It maintains speeds at levels you set (Technical terms explained Chapter 21). It is really only applicable on long motorway journeys. But it may be offered as standard equipment on higher specification models or a special edition you have on your list. It is a hidden cost (several hundred euros). Why buy when you don't need it? If a rival offers similar equipment without cruise control you could save hundreds.

Here's an indication of what items can cost
## Cars under 1400cc

| Item | Retail value € |
|---|---|
| ABS | 509 |
| Passenger and side airbags | 382 |

**Medium size family cars**

| (1400cc to 1900cc) | € |
|---|---|
| ABS | 480 |
| Traction Control / ABS | 789 |
| Fog Lamps | 121 |
| Heated Windscreen | 160 |
| Side Airbags 275.69 | |
| *ESP | 2096 |

*Electronic Stability Program (See Chapter 21) . Different prices for the same equipment are explained by higher VRT rates on cars with larger engines.

**TIP!** Pay close attention to what equipment you get as standard and what you want but have to pay for.

**Don't be a dipstick**

In most modern vehicles, the engine is encased so it can be difficult to find important checkpoints. But make sure you find the battery and, in the case of a second-hand car, check its condition, leads and connections.
Also find the oil dipstick (this is colour coded in newer cars) so you can easily and regularly check on oil levels.
When you eventually buy, read the brochure and handbook - regard it as the bible of the car - as carefully as you can. Hard to do in the excitement of it all, but worth browsing nonetheless.

**Service please**

Technological advances mean that service intervals are being extended all the time. See how they compare between different models. The longer the interval, the more cost effective.

**TIP!** Always buy the car that fits you best. And remember it's the little things that are most likely to annoy you on a daily basis.

**Pick and stick**

After conducting your Sit-In research, try to pick out three or four cars you feel most comfortable with.
Price is critical but even more important is being happy the car accommodates your needs as fully as possible.
**TIP!** Never lose sight of your initial spending budget. And continually remind yourself of what you need from your purchase.

**Some options: diesel or petrol?**

The two main advantages of diesel are economy and superior pulling power. These strengths are now complemented by so-called common rail technology (see explanation of terms Chapter 21) which makes them virtually as smooth and quiet as petrol engines.

However, petrols remain the main attraction because engines are smaller and less costly to maintain.

Diesels can cost upwards of €1,200 more than equivalent petrols. They also need more frequent oil and filter changes - all of which can negate their other economic benefits for average mileage drivers. But they can be real economic options for those who put up in excess of 20,000 miles a year.

**Manual or auto**

A minority of buyers opt for automatic rather than manual transmission. It makes driving easier, especially in heavy, congested traffic. As a general rule, automatics are useful if you have limited mobility, feel consistently uneasy with gear changing or drive a lot in gridlock conditions.

But an automatic transmission costs an average of €1,200 extra and automatics use upwards of 2% more fuel.

## Taking to the road - the real test

The 'fit' tests you carried out in the car in the showroom or dealership take on added importance when you get behind the wheel. This is where you get a true sense of the car and how you feel with and about it.

Try to take as varied a route as possible to see how it fares under the broadest range of everyday driving conditions you can find. A good salesperson/dealer will afford you plenty of opportunity. Take all the time you can. This is the drive that counts.

**Back seat drivers**

Also, try to bring along someone you know - but put them in the back. If you have rear seat passengers on a regular basis, it is important that they are comfortable too. A car can feel quite different from the back seat, especially on a long journey.

**The key elements you need to test**

How comfortable do you feel with, and in, it ?
How clearly and easily can you see the road in front?
How clearly can you see behind, via the interior and wing mirrors,

and the rear windscreen? If you have to strain or stretch to do so, you may have to put safety first and pass up this model. You simply must feel in control and fully aware of what is going on around you at all times.

Assuming you don't have a problem, the following will help:

**1.** How does the car feel on the road? Steady, easy to maintain in a straight line or heavy and difficult?

**2.** Is the cabin quiet? Is the engine noise subdued, noticeable or intrusive?

**3.** How well/badly does it absorb jolts and uneven sections of the road?

**4.** Do you notice tyre noise? – a little or a lot?

**5.** What is the radio reception like?

**6.** Does the steering wheel block your vision of vital instrument information?

**7.** Do you feel the front of the cabin is cramped when you have someone in the front passenger seat?

**8.** Are there are any squeaks from the dashboard area? Even at this stage there can be.

**9.** If it is a sunny day, is there much glare/reflection along the top of the dash/facia.

**10.** How easy is it:
to reverse? (be careful);
to change gears or brake?

If you have reservations about any items on the road test list and the dealer cannot put your mind fully at ease, you should consider looking at another model.

**TIP!** Always remember a car is a personal choice. If you do not like it, even for reasons you cannot define, don't buy it.

## Mind games

There will always be salespeople who try to get the upper hand psychologically. It is important not to be intimidated by such tactics.

The 'put down' is a famous trick and is designed to convey the imminence of a poor assessment of your car. After frowning over your car, they offer a price described as the 'very best' they can do, adding, perhaps, that the car is not a big seller and needs some work before being sold on. That may or may not be the case. But be aware this ploy can be designed so the shock of the initial low valuation softens you up for acceptance of a slightly higher, but still too low, second offer.

**The fightback**  That's where having an idea of ballpark values from the car ads, and/or asking a mechanic you know for average prices for cars like yours can equip you to deal with such people.
Usually, however, you are dealt with by professional salespeople who do a quick 'rekkie' and give a reasonable estimate.

**Busy signals**  If you are not happy with how a salesperson is dealing with you, or if you are left waiting for a long time before someone deals with you, let the manager or owner know.

TIP! If there isn't much between two garages on cost of change, it can come down to your own assessment of which is best for you.

## Chapter 10

# Buying secondhand

Buying secondhand can be a high-wire act without the safety net You have certain protections by law, but it does not mean you are insulated from potential loss.
Protection is even more limited when buying privately. In such cases, you essentially have to ask the right questions to get the correct information. It is not always volunteered.

**Check mate**  A car may have been badly crashed but the seller does not have to tell you. However, if you can prove it was dangerous and non-roadworthy when sold you could prosecute. But who wants that sort of trouble?
A growing number of dealers and distributors now have good used-car schemes which remove a significant element of risk. Cars in such schemes have been thoroughly checked and carry substantial guarantees. You may pay more but you stand to lose less.

**Secondhand price clues**  It is customary for a salesperson to ask how much you are thinking of spending. This saves them time and helps them provide you with a relevant choice of models. However, it can limit your scope. It might better suit your purpose to say you're after two/three/four-year-old version of a 4dr saloon, or 3dr hatch etc with a 1.4 or 1.6-litre engine - but that you are open to suggestions.

This gets you off the price 'hook' and offers the prospect of a much broader choice and price range.

**Play it again**

Many, if not all, the fit-and-feel checks outlined in Chapter 9 on buying a new vehicle apply to secondhand purchases as well.

**Who are you buying from?**

The next step is to check out the person, dealer or garage selling the car. Do you know them? Do you know anyone who has dealt with them? If buying privately from a stranger, be doubly careful. There is a higher risk of being duped, sold a shady, unsafe or stolen car.

**Trickery**

Stories of trickery abound. One of the best known is the car found to be the front of one and the rear of another. It passed several expert inspections before being discovered.

While most sellers and buyers are honest and legitimate, the danger is too great to accept anything at face value. Honest sellers/dealers will welcome queries.

<u>TIP!</u> Satisfy yourself about the other person's credentials before going any further.

**Check call**

If responding to an advertisement in the paper, get the person's full name when you phone initially.

Get a landline or office number and address.

Hang up if there's any hesitancy or fudging.

As a general rule of thumb, it is reckoned ads placed by private sellers tend to be a little longer as they try to give as full a picture as possible.

Those by dealers or commercial private sellers can be shorter and business-like.

**Match time**

It buying privately, try to meet the seller at his/her home, office or business. Ask to see the vehicle's documentation and service history as soon as you meet.

Check that the relevant data on the documentation - such as registration number, colour, model, body type (saloon, hatchback, estate etc) engine size, chassis number - correspond with those on the car.

**Day by day**

Don't inspect a car being sold privately in rain or twilight. Try to make sure it is at the seller's home or business and during daylight hours.

Dusk can hide a multitude. Many people 'look' at cars on their way home from work. If you opt for a quick initial impression at night, get the seller to take the vehicle to a well-lit area (such as a petrol station) or park it under a street light – this shows up uneven surfaces, dents and dints to great effect. But make no decision to proceed any further until you see the car in the clear light of day.

**Peace-of-mind guarantee**

Dealers, as opposed to private sellers, nearly always give a warranty or a guarantee. It can be from six months to two years - some on parts, and some on parts and labour.

Many offer extended warranties at additional cost. Just be clear on what is covered and for how long.

A warranty takes a lot of the risk out of buying second-hand. If possible, opt for a year's cover as six months is little time for something to go wrong.

Buying privately usually does not have such security.

**TIP!** You should keep one key question in mind when you view a used car for the first time, especially one being sold privately. Do all the elements in it 'fit' together or are there inconsistencies?

**Your First Check**

Obviously you can only pay for a professional engineering report once or possibly twice. Otherwise you end up spending your money checking rather than buying cars.

That's why the checks you carry out on your own are important. Many of those checks in the new-car 'fit and feel' test (Chapter 9) apply to secondhand cars too. A more detailed checklist is provided in Chapter 20. Hopefully the cars you're looking at have recently passed the NCT test and will be in reasonable condition overall. But a lot can happen to a car in three or six months. Recent research has shown that even two-year-old cars can have at least one potentially serious fault.

Based on individual cars, you may find some, or all, of the following helpful in coming to a conclusion about a car.

**Wear-and-tear zone**

Focus on the points where there should be visible wear and tear. Take your time. Don't be distracted by chit-chat or sales talk. Move around the car, slowly taking in as much as you can.

**The inside track**  The interior provides solid evidence of a car's wear and tear history. If there are indications of heavy use - torn seat fabric, frayed seat belts etc - it may be better to move on.
Big mileage clues also include discoloured headlining above the driver's seat, worn accelerator, brake and clutch pedals. Be extra careful of any car without a full service history.

**Round the houses**  Closely check that all lights, indicators, handbrake, horn, heater, air conditioner, radio, window winders, safety belts, door handles and locks are functioning properly. This only takes a minute or two but is recommended. The devil may be in the detail.

**Interior lights**  Check interior lighting, especially in the back and establish if the lights come on when the doors are opened.

**Mileage**  Is the engine noisy? Is there blue smoke from the exhaust? A 'yes' on one or both counts spells trouble.
Check the pedals on the brake, clutch and accelerator for wear. If they are bright-black new, they may have been replaced to give the impression the car has been less extensively used.
Speedometers that have been interfered with (clocked) often don't work properly. If you take the car for a drive, check that the needle moves smoothly. If it jerks or sticks it may have been tampered with. Take a close look at the mileage dial/odometer. Check if the digits to the left (in the thousands and tens-of-thousands columns) are even and not partially hidden. If they are, take care. An attempt may have been made to alter the mileage. For example 70,012 could have been 80,012 or 90,012. Clocking is prevalent in the UK. Be extra vigilant if buying from there.

**Inconsistencies**  Try to balance the wear in one section against another. Do the corners of the driver's seats, carpet condition, doorsill strike you as being compatible with a 45,000-mile, three-year-old car for example? If the pedals appear only moderately worn and the sills are frayed and tattered, you should be concerned.

**Panel games**  If the body panels do not visually line up, suspect it has been in an accident and not properly restored. If you wish, you can use a pen or pencil to compare gaps on one side with the other.

**In the shade**  Check under the bonnet, inside the boot, along the edges of doors, behind the grille, under the bumpers and boot lid for signs of rust or paint overspray. Is there any difference in either colour or shading of paintwork in these areas?

**Sweeping it under the carpet**

Lift any mats in the cabin or boot. They may be strategically used to cover up problems. Is there a smell of dampness or even mild mildew?

**Jack of all trades**

If the spare wheel is not in good condition, it suggests lack of overall care. Check there is a carjack and wheel removal tools. Are the jacking points worn or dinged? Be sure you know the points at which the jack should be fitted on to the car for safe hoisting if you buy.

**Battery**

The battery poles should be clean and clear of any white residue. If not, suspect the whole car has been neglected.

**Under cover**

Are there oil, or rusty water, deposits on the ground under the car? Suspect engine and/or radiator problems if there are.

**The ripple effect**

Look along each side of the car for ripples and uneven surfaces on the doors and wings. Paint that has been badly applied can look like the skin of an orange. It suggests carelessness.

**Handbook**

Again, make sure there is a handbook aboard. It is a car's bible and the best set of details about it you'll ever have.

**Previous owner check**

If you can, you should check with the previous owner about the car's history. Dealers and sellers of good standing will, if they have the previous owner's consent, give you the contact details. When you speak with that person, ask what sort of driving was involved and the number of miles on the clock when they sold it. Was it used to tow a trailer or a boat or a caravan? This may have implications for the clutch and rear suspension. If it is not possible to make contact, make sure you see the all the relevant documentation.

**Record deal**

The presence of a well documented service record speaks volumes for the authenticity of the car. Be wary if there isn't one. If there is, note the name of the last garage to service the car. If you wish, you can phone the service manager who should have a computerised record of servicing/repairs and might divulge their contents.

**Outstanding**   Always check to see if there financial commitments (hire purchase for example) outstanding.

**Belt it**   If buying from a dealer or garage, check when the timing belt was changed on any car with more than 50,000 miles on the clock. If it goes while you're driving, it is costly.

**Remember!** When you buy a used car you are buying the unused miles left in it and the consequences of previous abuse.

**A closer look**   If you are happy with your initial inspection of the car and feel comfortable with the seller, you can take an even closer look. But before taking it for a drive, make sure you are properly insured.

**Testing details**   And then you can give the car as detailed a check out as you like or think befits it. A thorough checkup, based on criteria used by the National Car Test, and a specially compiled checklist are detailed in Chapter 20.

The National Car Test compels every owner with a car aged four years and over to have it tested every two years. All cars of that age must display an NCT disc on their windscreens.

That instantly identifies those that have passed. Check expiry dates on the discs of any car you are considering. Try to buy something with at least a year, preferably longer, to its next test.

**TIP!** Walk away from any vehicle with which you have the slightest unease. First impressions tend to be correct.

**Leave to the experts**   When you are as sure of the car as you can be after checking as best you can, call in an expert to give the car a once over. Your regular mechanic may do this for you, or recommend someone else. Or you can use the services of the AA for example, even if you are not a member. Only employ someone you completely trust or who has been thoroughly recommended.

**Buying and selling privately**   Selling to someone you know is risky.

Buying privately in such circumstances can be equally dangerous. What happens if something goes wrong?

Unless they are in the trade, the seller will have no means of repairing the vehicle and getting him or her to pay for the repairs might be difficult.

People often buy cars they 'know'. They've heard it start next door every morning and know it never gave a day's trouble in three years.

But it is still advisable to get someone to examine it. It can also make sense to 'follow' such a car to the dealership where it is being traded in and buy it. The dealer will be delighted to sell it on quickly, and at a profit, once they've given it a check over. They'll charge you a bit more. But it may be worth it to have a year's warranty and access to repairs if something goes awry.

**First time, every time**

In a way we are all first time buyers because past success does not necessarily guarantee a favourable outcome in the future.

But for the first-time buyer, getting off on the right footing is essential. Buy a car with a sound safety record, a small, economical engine and a good reputation. Thousands of euros can be wasted in retrieving an initial mistake.

**TIP!** A smaller engine helps reduce road tax and general running costs. It affects insurance quotes too. When buying, bring someone along to help vet a potential purchase.

**In your favour**

One important factor favours the first time buyer.
You are unlikely to have a trade-in and are, therefore, a prized potential customer for a garage or dealer. They do not have to worry about getting rid of a trade-in. All buyers in such situations can, and should, exploit this. Obviously checks in Chapter 9,10 and Chapter 20 apply.

**Peace of mind**

If possible, go to a reputable garage where you have a comeback. If it is SIMI (Society of Irish Motor Industry) registered, it is accountable: you can have grievances heard and acted on.

**TIP!** Do NOT rush into buying. There will always be another option.

**Doing the deal
- Your Way**

When you are satisfied with a car, you can begin the discussion about price in earnest.
**1.** If you have noticed any faults, point them out to the seller. They should be taken into account in the price negotiations.
**2.** Establish what repairs you deem necessary and make sure the seller intends to carry them out. Be absolutely clear on this.
**3.** Then ask for a 'realistic' price and take your time considering it.
**4.** Do not consider meeting the asking price first time round and don't close the price gap too quickly

**5.** If the seller is reluctant to move on price, you may need to re-think. You can always say 'thank you' and leave.
If they refuse to budge much, take time out to think and assess, going over everything.
This can sometimes prompt a re-think on their part too, although they also have their cut-off point on the selling price.
Do not exceed your own valuation until you have given it considerable thought – away from the scene of the sale - and spoken with someone you trust.
A reputable salesperson, garage or private seller, will leave you a comeback route by allowing time for you to call them.

**TIP!** You can always bid upwards but it is difficult to lower your offer, so take your time spending your money. Approach the entire exercise on the basis that if you leave, they, not you, have missed out on a deal.

If the seller/salesperson comes back and reduces the asking price to within what you consider to be a bridgeable gap, do not jump at the opportunity immediately. In the case of a garage or dealer, see if they can offer something extra such as seat covers or a reduced price alarm to clinch the deal. If it's a private seller you can point out that, at this stage, a garage would be offering such items and you'd like an equivalent monetary gesture.

**Passing muster**

If you agree to deal and the outstanding items will be repaired, you can leave a deposit to secure it. Be absolutely clear on whether it is refundable or not. Insist on a receipt that is both dated and signed. Scrap the deal if a seller shies away from providing a written acknowledgement of your payment.
Later on, before you hand over the remainder of the money, check thoroughly that all repairs have been carried out. If there is work pending, withhold some of the payment until completion.

**Guaranteed to ease your worries**

Never buy secondhand from a garage or dealer without a good guarantee. Six months is an absolute minimum, a year preferable. Just be sure you understand what the guarantee or warranty covers. Parts and labour, or just parts? The distinction could mean a lot of money due to sky-high labour costs.

**Same car –
only different**

This sounds ridiculous, but it has been known to happen. Unscrupulous sellers will 'strip' a car of its more valuable items -- possibly worth hundreds of euros - and replace them with cheaper ones in the day or two it takes to 'put things right' before you collect your purchase. The costly items include alloy wheels, fog lights, special accessories, floor mats etc.

So make a written inventory of what was on the car you 'bought'.

**Chapter 11**

# Imports, auctions, rentals

Every year thousands of cars come on the market from the hire fleets. These 'newsed' (new-used) vehicles appear when the tourist season ends in the autumn.
Most are around six months old at that stage.
They have effectively been sold by distributors or dealers to finance companies for periods of between four and six months. The dealer/distributor is the registered owner but the finance company buys them and leases them on a short term agreement to the car rental companies. By prior undertaking, the dealer buys them back (at a lower cost of course) when the main tourism season ends and offers them for sale to the public.
They are often advertised as great bargains: this year's cars for thousands less than the new-car price.

**Rentals**  Some ads make it clear these are fleet rentals. Others do not. If buying any newsed car in the same year as it was registered, ask if it was a rental. Regardless of value and warranty considerations, rentals have had a variety and breadth of users and usage. Mileage can vary between 8,000 to 15,000 miles.

**TIP!** You should approach rentals as 'new' in terms of price, and the fit-and-feel tests already outlined. And treat them as secondhand in your search for flaws and damage.

Are they a good buy?
Do they represent good value?
Yes and No.

**The case for**

Yes, because you get a few months in a 'same year' car for upwards of €2,000-€2,500 less than the list price of six months ago. It will still have upwards of 18 months warranty left so there should be no real worries about having to pay for trouble in the medium term.

**The case against**

No, because price reductions may not always be as big as they seem. It can appear you are saving €2,000-€2,500 or more if you compare the 'giveaway' rental car price with the current new list price.

But, as we know, the list price of a new car can be subject to reasonable, small or no discount - depending on circumstances. Therefore it is possible you could have bought this car as new for a lot less than the current selling price suggests - for example in a straight cash deal, during a special promotion etc.

Secondly, your car will be a two-owner year-old in a few months and that will be reflected in its value next year.

The acceleration of depreciation could knock upwards of €1,200 off its value.

Thirdly, the period of warranty remaining may be only 18-months and not 30 months depending on the marque policy.

Fourthly, you don't know what the car has been through. It may have been subjected to heavy wear and tear both mechanically, and in the cabin/boot areas.

And think of all the suitcases jammed into boots, all the stopping and starting, children getting sick on back seats, cars revved hard, gears missed, clutches over used by drivers unfamiliar with gear change, and so on.

Dealers thoroughly check and valet these cars. Many rentals are in tip-top condition and mechanically excellent.

But you have to balance the following:

**For**  Reduced cost, still a new-ish car, still under warranty (usually at least 18 months left).

**Against**  Not such a low price, will be one-year old in a few months, is now second-hand, has had one owner, could have been harshly driven.

**Auctions: buying**  Cars are brought to auction for a variety of reasons.
It could be a bank/lending institution selling off repossessed vehicles, the trade shifting slow sellers, someone trying to sell secondhand to buy new in a 'straight' deal. Or, of course, someone getting rid of a bad car.

**Sold as seen**  Mostly, cars are ``sold as seen". That means they are sold with all their faults. There is no guarantee of their condition. You buy what you buy at the going rate. It could be a disaster or a bargain.

**Preview**  Usually you get a few of hours to view cars before the auction starts. Stickers in each car's window give its details and its 'lot' number. As a high proportion of vehicles come from fleet and leasing companies, you can expect them to have high mileage. But they are normally well serviced and maintained.
It is usual to pay a deposit prior to the start of selling. This gives you a bidding number or buying card and is refundable if you don't purchase.
The pace of an auction can be fast and furious. You need to familiarise yourself with this. Do not buy on your first visit to an auction. Pay one visit to get an idea of what cars are making. Carefully read the small print in the terms of business. You should not buy without an experienced mechanic or car expert vetting your potential purchase.
If you buy, you may have to pay a buyer's premium, which can cost upwards of €50. Some auctions require a sizeable deposit on purchase, and the remainder before you take the car.

**Bid on budget**  Set yourself a limit on what you'll spend and stick to it rigidly. The auctioneer's description of the car should include details of major damage and if part of the manufacturer's warranty is still current.

**TIP!** Be careful not to bid yourself into trouble.

**Sell**

To sell your own car at an auction you must fill in a form describing it, set a reserve price and deliver it with all its documentation some time in advance of the sale (previous evening for following morning auctions).

**Buying abroad**

If you decide to import a new or used car, be acutely aware that Vehicle Registration Tax (See Chapter 5 for a full explanation) plays a central role. There is an entrance fee.
If you buy a car for €5,000 in England and bring it back here, you MUST tell the authorities. You will not get road tax until it has been registered here.
And that involves the Revenue Commissioners deciding how much VRT will be charged.
They will value your import purchase on what they estimate it is worth on the Irish market NOT the market it is coming from.
They base their valuation on a huge database of existing Irish prices. For example, you may have paid the sterling equivalent of €5,000 for it. The Revenue may decide it is worth €8,000 here. You are obliged to pay the VRT based on their valuation (though you can appeal it later). The VRT on €8,000 adds roughly €2,000 to the price of your import, which now costs €7,000 landed here.

**TIP!** Do not fall into the trap of thinking you are going to be taxed on the price you paid abroad. You will be taxed on the equivalent Irish price.

**Faraway hills**

Something of a myth has grown up about the money to be saved by buying new or secondhand abroad.
Consider a number of factors before you go this route.
Unless you buy in left-hand drive, the nearest right hand drive markets are in Northern Ireland and Britain.
The sterling differential has for many years added considerably to the price of a car from these sources.
That makes it difficult to show a measurable saving after VRT.
If you do buy abroad, make doubly certain the vehicle has a current MOT certificate, though experience suggests, in many cases, even that is no guarantee of soundness.

**Europe**

Buying in Continental Europe is even more demanding on the pocket and shoe leather. You have the costs involved in getting there, staying for a few days, finding the car you like, bringing it

home and paying the VRT on its assessed Irish price.
All of this on a car that will most likely have left hand drive if secondhand, though you can order a right-hand drive model if buying new in these markets.

### Birthday

Secondhand imports come under the regulations that established the testing of private vehicles from January 4, 2000.
The birth date of the car - the day it was first registered in its country of origin - is the key. It means an NCT test is due on the anniversary date of first registration (once it is four years or older). Tests carried out in other jurisdictions are not accepted as an alternative. Its first registration determines its test date here.

### Far Eastern promise

On Japanese imports, mileage is usually quite low but usage may have been proportionately higher. With heavy, slow moving traffic in most Japanese cities, a car may have worked a lot harder than its mileage suggests. The wear and tear on clutch, gearbox etc in such circumstances can be disproportionate.
However, most Far Eastern and Japanese cars have a reputation for being well made and long lasting.

### Exocita

Be wary of buying 'Jap' import versions that have not been on sale in the general market here.
You need to be certain there are spare parts readily and easily available.
There can be a slight, but significant, variation between a part on a mainstream version and a subsequent model that was not on sale here.
For example a Toyota Corolla import could require one of six different size brake shoes.
Parts coming from Japan can be expensive and there may be a delay, during which time your car is off the road.

**TIP!** Buy Japanese import models currently, or previously, sold here by the Irish distributors. You stand a far better chance of getting parts. Usual checks apply.

### If you import you must:

Go to the Revenue Commissioners office nearest the point of entry and pay Vehicle Registration Tax (VRT). They will issue a Vehicle Registration Certificate, which will use a new Irish registration number. Get new registration plates fitted.
Go to an NCT (National Car Test centre) with the Vehicle Registration Certificate and have the vehicle's details put on the NCTS database. Then you can get the car taxed.

**Chapter 12**

# The cars, their sectors and why they might suit you

Cars come in all shapes and sizes - from tiny tots to motoring mammoths. It is easy to get confused with all the jargon. Based on body size, bodystyle, engine capacity, price range etc they are categorised by segment.

**What's in a name?**

What follows is a segment reference map which details these factors. It is designed to help you think about the sort of car that might best suit you.

Increasingly divisions between segments are blurred by new niche models which cover more than one.

Some cars crop up in more than one place because they straddle different segments.

**Microminis/city cars**

These are the smallest cars on the road. Also called little hatchbacks or 'hatches' they have no protruding boot. Engines are usually 1-litre (1,000cc) or under. Economical to run and relatively inexpensive to buy new. Popular second-hand with first time buyers, singles, or as a second-car family runaround. A good low-cost option to buy new instead of a larger used car. Remember engines make a difference for insurance purposes.

New car examples: *Daewoo Matiz, Daihatsu Cuore, Fiat Seicento, Ford Ka, Hyundai Amica, Seat Arosa, Suzuki Alto, VW Lupo.*

**Superminis**

So called because they are tidy hatchbacks but bigger than the original Mini. Wider choice of engines than microminis. As 3dr and 5dr vehicles, they can make good family run-arounds and will suit young single people or a mature couple trading down.

Stick with smaller engines (1-litre to 1.4-litre) if buying new as they are more economical and most in demand secondhand. There are now several small commonrail diesel engines available but they are expensive.

There are three sized-based grades within the sector.

Compact: Smaller cabins, 3dr versions are popular. Includes the Peugeot 106.

Midsize: Includes the Ford Fiesta, VW Polo, Citroen C3, Seat Ibiza, Opel Corsa, Nissan Micra, Toyota Yaris and Fiat Punto.

Larger: Includes the Skoda Fabia and the Daewoo Kalos.

Some manufacturers also offer saloon (booted) and estate versions of their supermini hatchbacks. The Skoda Fabia, Suzuki Liana, Daewoo Kalos and Seat Cordoba saloons are good examples. These nudge towards the small family car sector. Boot space can be particularly good.

The segment includes: *Citroen Saxo 2, Citroen C2 (from spring 03), Citroen C3, Daewoo Kalos 5dr, Daihatsu Sirion, Fiat Punto, Ford Fiesta, Honda Jazz, Hyundai Getz, Mazda 121, Mitsubishi Colt, Nissan Micra, MG Rover 25/ZR, Opel Corsa, Peugeot 106, Peugeot 206, Renault Clio, Seat Ibiza, Seat Cordoba, Suzuki Swift, Suzuki Ignis, Skoda Fabia, Toyota Yaris, VW Polo.*

**Small-family**

Noticeably larger than superminis, they come as 4-dr saloons, 3dr and 5dr hatchbacks and estates. Engines usually start around 1.2-litre and can range up to 2-litre in petrol and diesel, though special editions may be even larger. Prevailing engine size is between 1.3-litre and 1.4-litre. Boot space can vary substantially between models, so check.

Usually a large selection on the secondhand market. But equipment levels, styling and interior space vary greatly.

The line-up in this sector includes the *Alfa147, Audi A3, Citroen Xsara, Daewoo Kalos saloon, Fiat Stilo, Ford Focus, Honda Civic, Hyundai Accent, Kia Rio, Mazda 323, MG ZS/Rover 45, Nissan Almera, Opel Astra, Peugeot 307, Renault Megane 2, Seat Leon, Subaru Impreza, Suzuki Liana, Toyota Corolla, Volkswagen Golf, Volkswagen Bora.*

**Family/fleet**

These are larger, better equipped and more expensive 4dr saloons, 5dr hatchbacks and estates than in the previous segment. Many are bought by companies for business use. They are also popular with families.
The sector splits broadly into two sizes.
Compact: Large enough for everyday motoring, but not as roomy or expensive as larger family-fleet counterparts. Examples include the Hyundai Elantra, Seat Toldeo.
Medium-Large: Bought for company reps and by families. Newer models are noticeably larger and better equipped than their predecessors. Examples include the Toyota Avensis, Nissan Primera. Engine sizes tend to range between 1.6-litres and 2-litres petrol and diesel. Entry-level engine size for many marques nowadays is 1.8-litre petrol. Diesels are big sellers too with 1.9-litre a favoured size. Some are so roomy they also compete in the next (executive) segment. Examples include the Citroen C5, Ford Mondeo, Peugeot 406, VW Passat. Most engines range from 1.8-litre to 2-litre petrol and up to 2.2 diesel.
Thousands of petrol and diesel versions come on the secondhand market each year. Many have big mileage but those on lease-hire agreements with companies are usually well minded.
New-car examples include *Citroen C5, Daewoo Nubira, Fiat Marea, Ford Mondeo, Hyundai Elantra, Kia Mentor, Kia Shuma, Mazda6, Mitsubishi Carisma, Nissan Primera, Opel Vectra, Peugeot 406, Renault Laguna, Seat Toledo, Skoda Octavia, Toyota Avensis, Volkswagen Passat.*

**Small executive/fleet**

A varied segment, with a wide range of styles and body types. Engines mostly range from 1.6-litre to 2.5-litre, and fine diesels, their appeal lies in the mix of practical and luxury. Examples include the Volvo S40 (saloon) and V40 (estate). The Alfa 156, larger-engined versions of the Citroen C5, Ford Mondeo, Toyota Avensis, and Volkswagen Passat also compete.
They can be good value secondhand and provide an opportunity to get into roomy, well-equipped cars at reasonable cost.
The segment includes better equipped and larger engined versions of *Alfa 156, Citroen C5, Ford Mondeo, Mazda 626, Nissan Primera, Opel Vectra, Peugeot 406, Renault Laguna, Toyota Avensis, Volkswagen Passat* as well as the *Honda Accord, Hyundai Sonata, Mitsubishi Galant, Subaru Legacy,* and smaller engined versions of the *Audi A4, Volvo S40/V40.*

**Small executive/luxury**   Perception tends to divide this class into three broad categories
- the traditional 'big names' Mercedes Benz, BMW and Audi.
- the other luxury carmakers: Alfa, Jaguar, Lexus, Saab, Volvo.
- volume marques with luxury models such as Hyundai, Mitsubishi, MG Rover, Subaru.

The big names tend to have above-average prices and trade-in values. Values of others can drop more sharply and buying a three-year-old version can represent a bargain. These cars are generally well looked after by private owners or businesses.

Engines in this segment typically range from 1.8-litre to 3-litre but there are some larger, powerful variants.

The line-up includes: *Alfa 156, Audi A4, BMW Compact, BMW 3-series, Hyundai Sonata, Jaguar X-TYPE, Lexus IS200, Mercedes C-Class, Mitsubishi Galant, MGZT/Rover 75, Saab 9-3 Sport Saloon, Skoda Superb, Subaru Legacy, Volvo S40/V40, Volvo S60.*

**Medium executive/luxury**   Dominated by the big German marques and the Mercedes E-Class and BMW 5-series in particular.

Others in contention include Jaguar with its S-TYPE and larger-engined X-TYPE, Lexus with the GS range, Saab with the 9-5, and Volvo with the S80.

The emphasis is on safety and comfort. Good ranges of engine and trim/specification options.

All make good second-hand buys as you benefit from the value left after the first three or four years of the heaviest depreciation. Some fall in price far more sharply than others and represent real value. There are some exceptional diesel engines - the 3-litre commonrail diesel from BMW, the 2.2cDi from Renault, the D5 from Volvo are good examples.

Main contenders across the segment include: *Alfa 166, Audi A6, BMW 5-series, Daewoo Leganza, Hyundai XG, Jaguar X-Type, Jaguar S-TYPE, Kia Magentis, Lexus GS300, Mazda Xedos 9, Mercedes E-Class, Nissan Maxima, Opel Omega, Peugeot 607, Renault Vel Satis, Saab 9-5, Skoda Superb, Toyota Camry, Volvo V70, Volvo S80.*

**Large executive/luxury**   Between extras and larger engines, it is possible to end up paying more than €100,000 for one of these.

Big cars, big names here: Audi A8, *BMW 7-series, Jaguar XJ series, Honda Legend, Lexus LS430, Mercedes S-Class.*

All have extensive equipment and technology packages.

As second-hand buys, they represent perhaps the single most

attractive proposition in terms of value depreciation from new – relatively speaking.

Of course the sums involved are still large. But the difference between their new price and at three, four, five or six years can tempt a well-off value-conscious buyer. Naturally, they continue to depreciate but the level of loss is proportionately lower. Engines range from 2.8-litre petrols to 6-litres petrols and from 3-litre in diesel.

**MPVs/people carriers**

MPV stands for Multi Purpose Vehicle, but these are commonly called people carriers. They come in all shapes and sizes. Their attraction lies in their ability to carry up to eight passengers in high-driving comfort.

Some offer two rows of seats, others three and there are various arrangements which allow seats to be added, stored or removed. Some have seats that turn and swivel, others offer a choice of individual seats or a bench for the second row.

The ease with which the seating and luggage arrangements can be changed varies enormously.

Some have mechanisms that make it easy to fold seats, take them out or push them forward. Others are not so straightforward and may require heavy seats to be lifted out and stored. Ease of access and operation are essential criteria.

If buying secondhand, check for signs of heavy wear and tear.

**Mini MPVs/ mini-people-carriers**

This segment comprises tall, angular vehicles that create space vertically and provide room for four adults even though their wheelbases are often shorter than a supermini.

Most have excellent carrying capacity with the seats folded. Useful as city/town/school run-arounds. Compare prices carefully as some offer a lot more for your money than others. Engines typically range from 1-litre to 1.3-litre petrol.

*Daihatsu YRV, Opel Agila, Toyota Yaris Verso, Suzuki Wagon R+.*

**Small/midi people carriers**

Almost like small estates or tall hatchbacks, they slot between mini and mid-sized MPVs. This facilitates a high driving position and two, possibly three, rows of seats that can be changed around to cope with extra luggage.

They can be a versatile alternative to the small-family car though some, such as the Audi A2 and Mercedes A-Class are a good deal more expensive. As with the mini MPVs, check how easy it is to change the seating/luggage configuration. Engines usually range from 1.2-litre to 2-litre including fine small diesels.

Included here are: *Audi A2, Ford Fusion, Honda Jazz, Mercedes A-Class, Mazda Demio, Mitsubishi Spacestar, Opel Meriva (from 03), Peugeot 206SW.*

**Mid-size/compact people carriers**

These are more family-oriented vehicles with that long, semi-tall, rounded look. They can take four-to-five people in reasonable comfort. The most high-profile has been the Renault Scenic. Its success has spawned many competitors.

Opel took a most inventive step forward with the Zafira. It has three rows of seats but the rear row folds flat and easily into the floor to release extra space for luggage or shopping.

Size and price are the main distinctions across the sector.

Go for the value-for-money option. Some are priced too high for what they offer. And check that used models have not been put through the mill by previous users. Engines start at 1.4-litre and usually range up to 2-litres, with good diesels.

The line-up includes: *Chrysler PT Cruiser, Citroen Picasso, Daewoo Tacuma, Fiat Multipla, Ford C-Max (03), Hyundai Matrix, Kia Carens, Mazda Premacy, Nissan Tino, Opel Zafira, Renault Scenic, Toyota Corolla Verso.*

**Medium-to-large people carriers**

The Mitsubishi Spacewagon is probably the most familiar name in this segment. Seating capacity ranges from five to seven but luggage space can be restricted.

Some of the larger vehicles, such as the Hyundai Trajet, have made a virtue of better luggage space. Again, you need to be sure of seating configurations and previous treatment before buying. Engines typically begin around 1.6-litre and range up to 2.4 and the contenders here include the *Honda Stream, Hyundai Trajet, Mazda MPV, Mitsubishi Spacewagon, Toyota Avensis Verso.*

**Large people carriers**

These are large and roomy. There are two main groups. The principal models, such as the Ford Galaxy, VW Sharan, Chrysler Voyager are a mix of practical room and considerable comfort.

In the second grouping are the larger and more expensive Renault Espace, Toyota Previa and the Chrysler Grand Voyager. Vehicles across the segment will seat up to seven in comfort. Engines start with 1.9-litre commonrail diesels and can range up to 3.3-litre for the more luxurious versions.

Those competing here include the *Chrysler Voyager/Grand Voyager, Citroen C8, Fiat Ulysse, Ford Galaxy, Kia Sedona, Mercedes V-Class, Peugeot 807 (03-), Renault Espace, Seat Alhambra, Toyota Previa, Volkswagen Sharan.*

**Small coupes/ 'hot' hatches**

These two-door cars with sleek, sloped, crouching profile are bought for their looks and - sometimes - their performance. Some are highly specified versions of existing superminis or small-family hatchbacks. They usually have 1.6-litre to 2-litre high performance engines with sporty trim and body kit (bucket seats, rear spoilers etc). Expensive to insure, depreciation can be heavy.
Have the mechanicals thoroughly checked if buying secondhand. Models include: *Citroen Xsara Coupe, Ford Puma (off market 02), Opel Astra Coupe, Peugeot 206CC, Renault Megane Coupe, VW Gti, VW Beetle, MINI, MINI Cooper and CooperS.*

**Medium sized coupes**

Markedly stylish with blends of sharp lines and soft contours, their performance can vary from moderate to exhilarating.
As they fall into the motoring-for-pleasure bracket, they often pay lip service to practicality. Some can carry four passengers but rear-seat room is usually below average. Some are two-seater cars and designed to be nothing else. They often have turbocharged petrol engines, which can range from 1.8-litres upwards. Depreciation can be heavy after 3-4 years so second-hands can represent good value but check thoroughly for wear. And make sure you can park securely as they tend to attract attention.
Here you'll find: *Alfa GTV, Audi TT, BMW M Coupe, Coupe Fiat, Hyundai Coupe, Mercedes CLK Coupe, Opel Speedster, Peugeot 406 Coupe, Toyota Celica, Volvo C70.*

**Large coupes/ performance cars**

The same goes for these powerhouse status symbols. Engines range from 2-litre to 4-litre and even larger and capable of stunning performance, they are bought by those well-off enough to put their money where their motoring hearts are. Large engines - 4-litres - are common. Used values vary widely from extremely low depreciation to substantial value loss depending on market, cachet and availability.
Included here are: *BMW M3, BMW M5, BMW M Coupe, Jaguar XK8/R Coupe, Mercedes SLK, SL, CL, Porsche Carrera Coupe.*

**Remember!** You will never legally be able to fully exploit the prowess of many sports cars. These are made for stretches of German autobahn where speeds are unrestricted.

So buy them for the pleasure they can give in accelerating either from a standing start or within the gears and for their handling and ride qualities.

**Convertibles**

Many of the segments outlined above offer coupes with soft-top roofs (convertibles, cabriolets) that fold down for enjoyment on our intermittent sunny days. Despite the Irish weather, they are popular. Engines range upwards from 1.6-litres.

Getting the roof open and closed quickly is important and most now have electrics to speed the operation. Some have 'solid' hoods: they form a conventional 'metal' coupe roof when closed and fold into the boot when open.

A word of caution. Be careful where you park: soft-tops are vulnerable to malicious damage.

Convertibles of all sizes include the *Alfa Spider, Audi TT Roadster, Audi A4 Cabrio, BMW Z3, M Roadster, BMW Z4 Roadster, BMW 3-series Cabriolet, BMW Z8, Honda S2000, Jaguar XK8 Convertible, Lexus SC430, Mazda MX-5, Mercedes CLK, SLK, SL, MG TF, Opel Astra Cabrio, Opel Speedster, Peugeot 206CC, Porsche Boxster, Porsche Carrera Cabrio, VW Golf Cabrio, VW Beetle Cabrio (03), Volvo C70.*

**Wheels of power**

In four-wheel drive vehicles (4x4), all four wheels get a share of the power. In most small and medium sized cars, power usually goes to the front wheels while most large executive vehicles have rear-wheel drive. And some vehicles have All-Wheel-Drive where the power is distributed to each of the four wheels according to a range of conditions and loads.

Some buyers use their 4x4s to full capacity, but most passenger versions are driven exclusively on the road.

**Body building**

Some 4x4s/off-roaders are built in the traditional way – the body is bolted onto the undercarriage or ladder-frame. Land Rover's Defender is a good example. But a growing number of modern 4x4s and Sports Utility derivatives are built like a car: the body and undercarriage are made as one. This is called monocoque design. The Lexus RX300 and BMW X5 are examples of this.

**Large 4x4/Sports utility vehicles (SUVs)**

Big and strong, they are highly capable off-road and most, not all, are big comfortable travellers on the tarmac. Some, such as the Land Rover Defender are primarily workhorses but are fast becoming fashionable icons in their own right. Most are made for passenger comfort on and off the road, while some cater for the commerical 'van' buyer. Engines are predominantly turbodiesel and range upwards from 2.5-litres. They are sold as commercials (with solid panels where you'd expect rear side windows) and as passenger vehicles with side windows. Anything you buy in this segment needs a really serious appraisal because of the potential damage to the undercarriage, 4x4 technology and bodywork.
The big names include: *Chrysler Jeep Cherokee/Grand Cherokee, Isuzu Trooper, Mitsubishi Pajero, Range Rover, Nissan Patrol, Toyota Land Cruiser.*

**Prestige 4x4/SUVs/SAVs**

Their prime focus is on-road 'car-like' comfort though they have good off-road ability too. They are made to feel, look and drive like large luxury estates - with the added bonus of four-wheel-drive, and the cachet that goes with the marque.
All provide a depth of comfort on the tarmac. But, with the exception of the Range Rover, they do not measure up to the extreme off-road ability of more conventional 4x4s.
Lexus and BMW call theirs Sports Activity Vehicles (SAV) because of their monocoque construction. They are a relatively new breed. It will be interesting to see how they fare as secondhands. Petrols tend to be around 3-litres and there are some fine turbodiesels.
*BMW X5, Lexus RX300, Mercedes M-Class, Range Rover* are among the sector's big names.

**Medium 4x4/SUVs**

Many medium-sized SUVs have good off-road ability, but others are made for 'designer' 4x4 motoring i.e. they never leave the tarmac. Indeed some manufacturers offer two-wheel-drive versions in a realistic response to practical use. There are passenger and, usually less expensive, van versions with long (LWB) and short (SWB) wheelbases. Diesels predominate.
You'll recognise these by their muscular, sporty looks. They have good interior space. Commercial versions are the big sellers. Engines usually range from 1.8-litre/2-litre petrol to 2.5, 2.7, 2.9, 3-litre turbodiesel or larger.

The second-hand market is a specialised area and you need expert assessment on a vehicle-by-vehicle basis.

Contenders for your new-vehicle money include the *Hyundai Terracan, Land Rover Discovery, Mazda Tribute, Nissan Terrano II, Opel Frontera, SSangYong Rexton (distributed by Daewoo).*

### Compact SUVs

These are nicely sized, easy to get around in and can be fun. Emphasis is on 'lifestyle' and car-like qualities. Engines range upwards of 1.6-litre in petrol and 2-litre turbodiesel.
These SUVs are a good option as secondhand buys but remember any mechanical faults on a 4x4 can be costly to repair. Examples include: *Honda HR-V, Honda CR-V, Hyundai Santa Fe, Jeep Wrangler, Land Rover Freelander, Mazda Tribute, Nissan X-Trail, Subaru Forester, Suzuki Grand Vitara, Toyota RAV4.*

### Mini-SUVs

These are designed with the 'active' urban driver in mind. Engines are usually small and start at 1.3-litres
Not too many around - the *Daihatsu Terios II* and *Suzuki Jimny* are the chief exponents.

### Twin-Cabs

A recent big-selling sector due to a quirk of Vehicle Registration Tax. In basic form, these pickups have a cab with two rows of seats and a flat cargo/load area. They have attracted a low rate of tax for some time and prices to the public have been reduced by thousands of euros in many instances. They're great fun and practical to a point, but there isn't that much room in the cabin, especially the back seat/bench.
However, the reduced VRT price makes them a real alternative and good value. Varieties include the *Ford Ranger, Mitsubishi L200 Twin Cab, Nissan Pathfinder Double Cab, Isuzu TFS Crewcab, Mazda B-series Pickup, Toyota Hilux, VW Crewcab.*
Also qualifying for the €50 VRT charge are the *VW Transporter Crewcab, Kia Sedona, Renault Trafic and Master, Opel Vivaro and Movano, Fiat Scudo and Ford Transit.*

### Varied market

The second hand market for 4x4s and SUVs varies widely. With so much technology involved in four-wheel-drive there is no substitute for buying reputably so check out your nearest 4x4 dealer.

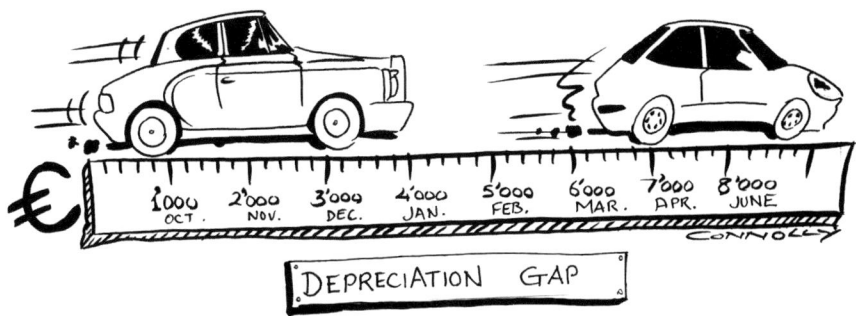

## Chapter 13

# Appreciating depreciation

**Where to look for and pick up on the bargains**

The bigger the secondhand car, the better the potential for a secondhand bargain. All cars lose most value in the first year. Most large models are notorious for their rapid rate of depreciation.

Our research shows that some large luxury vehicles can fall in value by an average of €12,000-a-year and more over the first three years from new.

And some family/fleet cars can lose upwards of €6,500 over two years when high mileage and market conditions combine to depress values. Even well known names such as the original Ford Mondeo and Citroen Xantia fell in value by such amounts while others, such as the Fiat Marea, suffered greater depreciation. Smaller cars have tended to fare better in the depreciation stakes as traditionally there has been a consistent level of used-car market demand for them. But the high volume of small-car/supermini sales in 2000 put a lot of pressure on values as there was little interest in the trade-ins against them and used prices plummeted. As the new cars filtered back onto the market, values had steadied but at a lower level, so depreciation levels were high.

The depreciation period taken here is over three years. The figures attempt to provide a guide to normal value trends over such a timespan and not to overly reflect the effects of the distortion caused by the 2001 price meltdown - though of course it has to be factored in.

**Microminis/superminis**  These hit really affordable levels after three years. Cars costing €12,000 new can dip to €6,000 (50% depreciation) and lower in that time. Better regarded models can hold falls to 40%. So much depends on market perception of individual model and maker, mileage and condition.

**Small family cars**  Average depreciation here is between 45%-55% over three years but can be higher. Again it depends so much on make, model and condition. This and the following sector are particularly sensitive to how 'new' the car is when you buy. The imminence of a new arrival could knock another €1,000 to €1,500 off the used price of a current model.

**Family/fleet**  Previous use has a marked effect on secondhand prices here – a busy fleet life or a sedate family history can make a huge difference to values.
Depreciation can range from 40%-60% (and more in cases of high mileage and replacement with new model etc). Insist on service records for all cars but especially those from this sector. This is where mega mileage can be piled on.

**Smaller executive/fleet**  Much the same levels of depreciation apply in this category where big mileage is not unusual. A well-minded model with reasonable mileage can offer several years of good service. And the heaviest depreciation has been endured by someone else. The shorter life cycle from new-car-to-new-car means these can be quickly overtaken by fresh models and used-car prices can be hit.

**Small executive/luxury**  Depreciation fluctuates widely from as little as 30% for exceptional pristine, scarce, big-name versions to 55%+ for less well-known cars. The latter can be great buys as they suffer unduly from their lack of 'snob' value.

**Medium executive/luxury**   And the same applies here. They take a fair hit in the first three or four years, but the better-known hold above-average values. Usually well cared for, they can make good secondhand buys especially if you plan on holding onto one for a long time because they tend to have the build, equipment and technology to last. Some can have high levels of equipment which previous owners added from new. But as additions count for less as the years pass you could get a top-spec motor for little above the average price.

**Large executive/luxury**   They suffer huge depreciation – by initial annual amounts that would buy a brand new family car. For example a car costing €95,000 new, could lose nearly half its value in three years, our research found, depending on mileage and condition.
Buying a four or five-year-old version is one way of beating the heavy depreciation trap and gaining an excellent car. But don't forget its value shedding days are not over. Great cars to own but expensive on depreciation and running costs.

**Sports cars/convertibles**   A few of the more sought-after luxury performance versions retain values remarkably well - while others plummet. Because of their potential performance they need the most rigorous checking for damage and worn mechanicals. A good one can be real value as a three-year-old.

**People carriers: tiny tots to crowd pullers**   These are popular secondhand and, whether tiny, mid size or large, you can expect most to have had reasonably full working lives – bringing children to school, taking the family away etc. Condition is everything - from mini-MPV to large luxury people carrier - and depreciation follows accordingly with 45%-55% of original new price a good guide for a three-year-old.
More than all other cars, the rear seats and boot/luggage area come in for a lot of through traffic. Check too that the medium-sized ones, in particular, have not been used as taxis.
Well-minded three-year-old versions represent a good prospect but make sure they accommodate you/your family's needs for seating, luggage and ease of access. Don't fall prey to the big-car-for-the-money temptation - they can depreciate more quickly - if you only need a compact five-seater. The latter tend to be in keener demand because they are so convenient as family-type cars and relatively economical to run.

**Traditional 4x4s**

Because they are such highly specialised vehicles, you simply must buy from a reputable garage or private outlet. Like people carriers, previous usage determines their value secondhand, but you need expert opinion on hand to make sure there is no trouble lurking in all that four-wheel-drive technology.

What you can't know is how heavily they have been worked. The state of the bumpers can give good clues. If the underside of the front area is scratched and dented, the vehicle may have taken a heavy pounding. Dents and loose mountings on the rear bumper can also give a good clue to its workload.

**SUVs**

Most of these are used as everyday on-the-road saloons so they are less likely to have come in for a severe hacking. Competition in this sector is keen. Smaller ones are often only used as stylish town cars and are most unlikely to have ever towed anything. Larger ones may have had a horsebox, boat or caravan on tow at some stage but they're unlikely to have had to endure heavy punishment. Evidence of even moderate off-road use can knock quite a few hundred euros off a three-year-old's value.

As with virtually all cars, the amount lost in depreciation is larger with the bigger ones, though some of the medium sized, trendier versions have managed to hold decent values. Previous use is critical. The key areas to watch out for are the rear bumper for signs of towing.

And check on uneven tyre wear (costly to replace on these). This may suggest chassis misalignment or constant use over rough ground or heavy, careless driving.

**Remember!** The rate of fall in the value of a car is in direct proportion to the level of risk perceived by dealers in taking it and using it, or passing it on to someone else.

Quality will win in the long term and a good reputation is most often earned through producing the goods year after year, for customer after customer.

**Extra, extra – there's little gain**

Being tempted by an alluring 'extras' package can be a costly exercise in the long term. All the evidence suggests 'extras' diminish greatly in value during the first few years of your new car's life. You will get very little in return when you trade in.

So enjoy them and use them for your benefit but do not expect them to yield a financial return when you sell.

Their cost depreciates more quickly than the basic vehicle package. It is estimated that €1,000 worth of extra equipment can dwindle to as little as €100 over 36 months.

Basic versions of cars are euphemistically called 'entry level' in the trade. Their equipment is standard across the range but it can be skimpy at this level as distributors prune costs to maximise price competitiveness. Many buyers opt for higher equipment versions.

Ironically, having electric windows, power steering, anti-lock brakes etc (See Chapter 21) as part of a factory-fitted package usually costs less than if you had to buy and add each individually. And while extras may not pay, they can add enjoyment, safety and comfort as well as helping to sell your car more quickly.

**Colour**

Colour can impact on the value of your car second-hand. Stronger primary hues such as red, black, green and blue tend to do best. Silver has been the popular colour of recent years.

**Tyres**

You should give tyres on any car you're thinking of buying a close look. The legal minimum tread is 1.6mm - about the width of a 5 cent coin - but you should consider changing well in advance of that.

Most new cars have a recognisable tyre brand name fitted. Three companies - Bridgestone, Goodyear and Michelin - supply 70% of original equipment tyres for new cars worldwide.

However, worn tyres are often replaced with an alternative brand. That's no problem so long as they are all the same. There can be a big difference in quality and performance. Tyres can be expensive but they are your only contact with the road and worth the best investment you can muster.

Make sure the tyres on a secondhand car are all the same size, and that they meet with the manufacturer's recommended size and speed rating. You should find these in the car's handbook. Larger tyres are promoted for their handling and performance advantages by carmakers. But they also cost more to replace. Really low-profile tyres are usually less comfortable on poorer roads.

**MPG and emissions**

Most dealerships now have facts and figures on each new car's fuel consumption and emissions on prominent display. They provide a good basis for comparison on this aspect of running costs.

Chapter 14

# The good, the bad and the ugly

These are some general pointers on models worth considering and those to be avoided in your search for a car. In the main it applies to used cars but, as you'll see, most new ones also come indirectly into the reckoning.

**What to buy and what to avoid**

It is important to remember that use/misuse, type of driving/work, number of drivers, region of country, age and regular/absence of servicing all play major roles in determining the condition, suitability of, and demand for, a secondhand car.
So while these comments are intended to help you avoid the pitfalls, the checks and balances outlined in Chapters 9 and 20 also need to be applied to individual vehicles.
As a rule of thumb, the models under consideration are mainstream cars up to seven years of age - in alphabetical order. With some exceptions, they are reviewed upwards from the smallest model made by each manufacturer to the largest or most exotic. Dates for the main revamps/revisions, updates and brand new arrivals are given so you can check on the exact model you are looking at.

**Alfa Romeo**

Maker of lovely cars with crisp performance, it suffered until the late nineties from an old lineup. The arrival of the compact executive 156 range transformed its fortunes and perception, and subsequent models have built on that.

The advice is: Stick with older versions of the new arrivals rather than dip into later editions of their predecessors.

That's why **145** small-family 3dr hatchback and 5dr **146** (96-00) should be left to the era they belong - when Alfas were nowhere near as good as they have been from 1997. The old Boxer engines (pre-96) in those cars were only moderate. Better Twin Spark engines started in 1996 but there are still better options secondhand.

The mid-size **155** (- 97) was no great shakes in its day and is now completely overshadowed. Far better options elsewhere.

The **147** (Dec 00/effectively Jan 01) is a great little Alfa with a lot of style and pace, yet roomy enough to make a small-family option. Nice used buy.

Buy **156** (97/effectively for 98 market) versions from 98 onwards. This award winner got a subtle but significant revamp in 02. A new JTS engine series was added and will eventually replace the entire Twin Spark engine line-up. This is a fine innovative car, with exceptional handling, great looks and is a stylish buy new or used.

The new **166** luxury car (Jan 99 -) completely outclasses what was a reasonable predecessor, the **164** (up to 97), although it lacks real sparkle and trails the 147 and 156 in appeal and style. But it is value as a used buy.

The **GTV** (95 -) coupe and soft-top **Spider** (96 -) are stylish and good to drive. You should be able to pick one up at reasonable money. Check for signs of over-zealous driving and heavy wear. New models late 03.

**Audi**

Well made, resilient and in demand secondhand, Audis tend to last well. The sparkle they often lack when new can become an asset of longevity second-hand. Their quality build appears to withstand the poundings dished out by our roads better than most.

The **A2** (Sept 00) is an innovative small aluminium hatch-cum-mini-MPV that competes in the same segment as the Mercedes A-Class. Expensive new, it may be more affordable as a two or three-year-old. The 1.4-litre diesel is particularly frugal but expensive. Great little car but costly.

The **A3** (96 -, 5dr added late 99, restyled late 00) is also pricey new but worth considering as a three or four year old. You could get a reasonable deal on what is a solid but overpriced car when new.

The old **A4** small executive (95-01) is highly regarded as a solid, roomy vehicle that copes well with our poor quality roads. The 1.6-litre petrol is a good economic option. The new version (01 -) has much improved handling and cabin space.

The **A6** (- 97) was a big, uninspiring medium executive motor. Its replacement (July 97, revised 01) is much better with the 01 upgrade making a significant difference. Use knowledge of this to get a better deal on pre-01 versions. Big roomy car.

The **A8** (94 -) is a large luxury aluminium vehicle, which has its own small but loyal following. Very much a niche product, but an interesting buy secondhand. New one (03).

The **TT Coupe** (May 99 -) and **Roadster** (Jan 00 -) represent real flair in two-seater motoring. The Coupe is likely to be more popular secondhand and a good buy - usual checks apply.

## BMW

For many, the name is synonymous with sporty driving. The cachet underpins higher-than-average used values though the old 7-series was not spared the reality of depreciation in its sector. Specification in older Beemers was poor for so-called executive cars. Newer versions are much better equipped. Pay older secondhand prices accordingly.

BMW has had a policy of trying out new engines in existing models first. So you can pick up cars immediately previous to new or current vehicles with a new-era engine in them.

The old **Compact** (94-01) was a sawn-off 3-Series with a dated rear suspension. Not great really, but much sought after secondhand. The new one (01- ) is substantially better - and that gives you something to bargain with for older models.

The **3-series** proper (up to 98) had saloons, estates (called Tourings) and coupes in an extensive range. They remain popular, with some of the best residual values on the market.

The new 3-series (Oct 98-) went on sale while old-model versions of other bodystyles continued for a time. These were gradually replaced by new versions over the subsequent 18 months or so. Check on which version you are looking at.

One problem with the 3-series in particular is the confusing badging: 316i denoted 1596cc and 1895cc engines at different times; 318i (1796cc and 1895cc) and 323i a 2494cc engine. They changed engine sizes but not the badging. Ask on a car-by-car basis.

The **5-series** (96-03, several revisions/equipment upgrades) has been a major player in the luxury segment since the early nineties. The new 5-series is a late 2003 debutant.

A well-minded 5-7-year-old 5-series can be a good buy. The car has been consistently described as the best production vehicle in the world. Buying newer is better for equipment purposes.

At the higher end of the market, all prestige cars tend to trail off in value quickly after four or five years so you could get a real bargain **7-series** (94 –01, several revisions; brand new car 02) for example with a lot of equipment and an excellent engine. The same goes for the exotic **8-series** (-97).

The **Z3** (Mar 1997 -, revised Dec 99, new **Z4** spring 03) is a little runaround roadster of smart disposition. As with all roadsters, check on condition of soft-top roof for signs of leakage. The **M Coupe** is an absolute tearaway - great car but of limited value on our roads. Z4 roadster represents a move up market with greater emphasis on performance.

The **X5** (00- ) is a large luxurious Sports Activity Vehicle (SAV) with particularly good road handling and moderate 4x4 capabilities. It is primarily designed for use on the tarmac. Initial scarcity of new models will maintain good secondhand values. A desirable, if expensive, buy.

**MINI, Mini**

BMW now owns **MINI** (July 01-). Variants include the nippy Cooper and the more recent CooperS (02-). Initial demand suggests plenty of buyers secondhand despite big price for a small car.

Old (pre-BMW) **Minis** will always have their enthusiasts and buyers but were severely overpriced for what they offered near the end of their era.

## Chrysler

Don't buy any pre-2002 **Neon**s (96, off market 01) unless the asking price is exceptionally low. And, even then, consider it reluctantly. This was an old car in new clothes from day one and the 2-litre automatic only had a four-speed gearbox. It was poor and thirsty. Its main attractions when new were low price and good equipment levels. There are far better alternatives.

The larger people carrier, **Voyager** (97-01), is a real proposition if you're in the market for a good used one. But the new version (01- ) is a big improvement on older versions. That knowledge should benefit your deal if buying a pre-2001 model.

## Chrysler Jeep

The marque is famous for its Jeep **Wrangler** (97-01) an individualistic American 'original'. A niche product, it is always in demand secondhand.

The **Cherokee** (93-02, new 2002-) and **Grand Cherokee** (1996, revised 1999, CRD diesel added May 02) are of the big, powerful, plenty-of-room-and-comfort school of motoring. The new Cherokee is far smarter looking and better to drive. The scarcity of diesels in previous versions is a drawback. Petrols were/are large and thirsty. Bargain on that basis.

The **PT Cruiser** (01 -, CRD diesel added 02) is a striking, retro-looking people carrier/estate, certain to attract interest as a two or three-year-old because it is so radical and practical. Initial scarcity should support prices so you may have to pay a bit more for this.

## Citroen

Avoid the dated **AX** supermini ( -97) which was replaced by the Saxo.
Older versions of the **Saxo** (96 -, revision 99) are also overshadowed by far superior newer small cars from this manufacturer. Later Saxo models are well equipped but there are better options both within the marque and outside it.

Examples of these are the innovative **C3** (02-) which effectively replaced five-door Saxo versions and the **C2** (03-) which replace three-door versions. Good used buys in prospect here.

The small-family **ZX** (91-97) is also dated now. Much better to go for its successor, the **Xsara** (97- , revamp in 00). This is underrated with equipment levels making secondhand prices attractive.

The family/fleet **Xantia** (93, major revamp 97) was replaced by the C5 in 01. It had dated rapidly in its last few years and you should benefit on price from that. Diesels are best. Bargain hard here.

The **C5** (01 - ) is a well-equipped, user-friendly large family/fleet car. Plenty of cabin space. Diesels excellent. Will make a decent secondhand buy in terms of room and equipment.

The old **XM** executive (- 99) was a great drive, hugely roomy and extremely comfortable, but notorious for its poor residual/trade-in values. Not too many around. Buy at rock bottom money only – and then enjoy a great old car.

The best known of Citroen's people carriers is the **Picasso** (00 -), a well-equipped, usefully roomy mid-sized MPV. Should be good secondhand value in a competitive market.

Then there's the quirky but practical **Berlingo Multispace** (97-, revised late 02 for 03 market). Go for later 5dr (00-) versions (two conventional front doors, two sliding rear doors and rear door) rather than older 3drs as it was difficult to access rear seats. Based on a van, there's plenty of room. Well priced new, it is a different, practical buy.

The large people carrier **Synergie** (96- ) is like so many others - comfortable, roomy and accommodating. Nothing outstanding. Not many around. Alright if the money suits. Successor, the **C8** is an 03 debutant.

**Daewoo**

The marque made a big impression when it arrived at the start of the fast-growing 1999 market. But subsequent trading difficulties at the parent company undermined market perceptions.
The parent company has now been taken over, by General Motors (Opel), heralding a more settled outlook.
These are straightforward cars. Well priced new and secondhand. New additions, the **Rexton SUV** (02) and **Kalos** supermini/small saloon (Oct 02) further expand the range.

The city car **Matiz** (99, revised 01) mixes economy and space in a modern bodystyle. It has the makings of a good purchase secondhand - at the right money.

The **Lanos** small-family car (99, minor revision 01, replaced by **Kalos**, (Oct 02) also sold well. It's unfussy and bland, so bargain hard when buying secondhand.

Expect good used-car value from the mid-size **Nubira** (99, new model 00) especially the smarter-looking estate. Bargain hard on these.

The mid-size MPV **Tacuma** (01) is a compact vehicle with good equipment levels. Its original 1.8-litre engine was thirsty, and replaced by a 1.6-litre in 02. Make sure you use that to drive a better deal if considering an earlier version.

The executive **Leganza** ( 99-) also looks like being a good secondhand buy. It has plenty of equipment, was well-priced new and, considering it is new to the executive segment, it should be even better secondhand. Lack of 'snob' value will be good for your pocket if buying secondhand.

**Daihatsu**

There are not many models around because they were effectively off the market for some time before being re-introduced in 1999. If you have a good local dealer, these cars can represent a thrifty, economical option as epitomised by the gone but not forgotten Charade.

The city car **Cuore** (99, new 03) and supermini **Sirion** (99, new 03) are few-frills models that provide basic value-for-money options at a competitive end of the market.
The current models won't win styling awards but they can be practical used buys because their new-car pricing is keen.

The **YRV** (00 ) is a 5dr mini MPV with a high driving position and good interior space. Good around town. A practical buy secondhand, it should come on the market at reasonable money.

The Sport Utility/4x4, **Fourtrak** (revised version 95, discontinued 01) is well regarded in the trade. It has the quality to give plenty of service at a reasonable price.

The **Terios II** (99, revised May 01) is an option as a small 'trendy' urban 2WD or 4WD to compete with the Suzuki Jimny. Again price should be a strong attraction. Revision made a big difference, so make sure earlier model values reflect that if buying.

## Fiat

A big sales surge in the boom years means there are plenty on the secondhand market. Their smaller cars are better sellers than their larger ones - and are keenly priced.

The **Cinquecento** (91-95; new range 95) microminis are popular despite improved new-new **Seicento** successor (97-). The latter is a perky little city car and a good buy secondhand, at the right money, for town use in particular.

Older **Punto** (93-99) superminis are still popular and can be really well priced. New Puntos (late 99, effectively 00 -) are more stylish, roomy and have some of the best equipment levels in their class. Good pricing new - and there are plenty on the secondhand market.

Older versions of the small-family **Bravo** 3dr or **Brava** 5dr (late 95-01) are good driving, nice-looking cars but only recommended if you get a great deal. They failed to make the impact expected. Their secondhand values reflect that now and are likely to do so in the future. There are better options, though prices may be tempting.

They were replaced by the **Stilo** (Jan 02) a small-family car with exceptional levels of standard equipment. But it competes with some of the best known cars in the world for your money. Fiat's previous lack of success in this segment has muted sales.

There are newer and better options on the market than the **Marea** station wagon (96-). It is roomy and a lot of new car for the price but dated, and not Fiat's best by a long way.

The **Coupe Fiat** (93 as 1.8, 2-litre) was an exciting sports car. But try one with the newer 5-cylinder 2-litre 20-valve engine (96 -). They drive well and secondhand prices are keen.

The mid-size people carrier **Multipla** (99 -, revamp June 03), is as unusual as it is practical. With two rows of seats it accommodates six. You love it or hate it. The diesel is well worth considering.

**Ford**

The large people carrier **Ulysse** (94-, new late 02) was not spectacular when new. Part of a joint venture with PSA (Peugeot/Citroen) it was essentially a Citroen Synergie/Peugeot 806 by another name. The arrival of its successor in late 2002 is another good reason to hold out for a better deal on older versions.

The 3dr city car **Ka** (96-, new engines/editions 03) took a while to get established. But it's a good used buy as a city motor. It's neat, nippy and easy to park.

Older **Fiesta** models (-99, revised 99, new 02) are fine if you go for something later in the nineties. Try to buy one with the 1.25i Zetec engine. It's much better than the staid 1.3-litre. It may cost a little more but it's worth it. Ask specifically which engine is under the bonnet. Plenty of choice. New car much roomier, better all round. Fiesta-based **Fusion** midi-MPV arrived autumn 2002.

Avoid older **Escorts** (last generation from 95). They are poor options now. Early versions were buried by subsequent revamps, improvements and additional equipment which weren't anything to write home about either.

And all were washed out by their small-family replacement, the excellent **Focus** (98-01, update early 02) whose secondhand versions should most definitely be on your shortlist in this small-family-car sector. The 02 revamp changed the look of the front and added some equipment. Excellent buy secondhand and use the revamp knowledge to your advantage. This is a big seller and there should be a good selection.

The previous family/fleet **Mondeo** (93, revised 96) was a decent car, and handled well, though it dated quickly. It was heavily revamped in 1996. The new car (00-) is a significant improvement all round and much more spacious. Go for 96+ versions of old model if buying it secondhand. They're roomier in the rear and far smarter in appearance. Rear light clusters and other subtle changes made a big difference. Avoid big mileage versions. These were popular cars with sales reps as well as families.

The original **Galaxy** people carrier (95-, revised 00) was, like so many others of its ilk and era, moderate - with lots of plastic in the cabin and dashboard. It was transformed by a 00 revision.

That should help you get a better deal on an older one. But, if you can afford to, you'd be better off to go for the new one. It has a lot more to offer in every respect.

The **Puma** (97 -, off market 02) is a Fiesta-based sports car that is well worth looking at. It has brilliant handling and is a delight to drive. A fun buy secondhand.

The old 'executive' **Scorpio** (94, off market 99) looks completely dated now. Don't touch it unless you really want one for its room/equipment and you get it for a truly exceptional price.

The **Probe** (94, off market 97) coupe never took off; don't bother unless it's particularly well priced.

The **Cougar** (98-01) is a marvellous looking large coupe but disappointing to drive. Few around. Bargain hard.

The **Explorer** (-01 off market) is a big gas guzzling American Sports Utility. But it's costly to run and there are better options.

The **Maverick** (93 -, off market 98) was a joint venture vehicle with Nissan, which badged its version the Terrano. Tall and muscular, it competed in the same segment as the Opel Frontera. Worth a check.

**Honda**

In the main, Hondas have a good name which is reflected in strong prices new and used.

The **Jazz** (02-) is an innovative town car with mini-MPV qualities and is a recommended buy when it comes on the secondhand market.

Older Civic (95-00) and large-family/small executive Accords (95-98) can be fine used-car buys - they're well built - although some Civic 2drs are overrated and overpriced.

The older **Civic** 4dr is larger than the 5dr. It was made in Japan while the 5dr was made in England. The latter is not nearly as spacious. But secondhand models of the new 4dr/5dr (early 01, 3dr late 01) have the room and style to be good family purchases for a long time. The 5dr is MPV-like and roomy; the 4dr is more conventional. The 5dr is more appealing.

The large family/executive **Accord** (late 98 - ) is an accomplished, if bland, car and a good second-hand option. Its blandness detracts from superb engineering - that will benefit your pocket when buying secondhand. New car (03-) is much better looking.

The **CR-V** (97, new 02) is a refined mix of sports utility and people carrier. It has realtime 4x4 which means it uses front wheel drive most of the time but can power all four wheels if extra traction and grip are needed. The new model is larger and better all round. Previous one was good and well worth a look.

The **HR-V** (99, revised 02) is a striking looking, individualistic Sports Utility-type vehicle. Hugely popular since its arrival. Highly regarded new and used. Good residual values mean few bargains.

The **Integra Type-R** (98-, off market 01) is a high-performance car with considerable capabilities. Watch out for evidence of heavy previous driving.

The **S2000** (Mar 00-) is another performance highflier with stunning looks. Few on the used market.

The **Prelude** (97 - off market 01) is an understated coupe. Could be a good used buy if previously well treated because it is more of a subtle sports car than an ostentatious performer.

The **Legend** (97 - ) is a large, luxury car of classic Japanese efficiency with little visual appeal. Depreciation levels in its sector should make it an excellent used buy. Boring but good value, though very few on the used market.

The **Shuttle** (96-01) was one of the best large MPVs of its generation. Replaced here by Civic-based **Stream** (late 01). The former is a good buy if you can get one, the latter has the potential to be an even better purchase.

**Hyundai**

Avoid models before 1995. Since then the range has been completely overhauled and massively expanded and a new Irish distributor has been appointed. The new crop epitomises value-for-money motoring.

The tall and angular micro-MPV **Atoz** (98 -00 ) is one of the more unusual offerings – so much so Hyundai toned down its strange outline and introduced the more conventional Amica city car in late 99. If buying an older version, bargain hard on this basis.

A new supermini, the **Getz** (Nov 02 -) adds even greater depth to the range and follows the marque's value-for-money tradition.

Older **Accents** (95-, new one 00) and **Lantras** (late 95 –00) are reasonably good second-hand buys. Check for condition and test drive over a variety of road surfaces. Good as three, four or five year olds.

Hyundai pricing has been competitive so you should benefit from that on the second-hand market too. New versions of the Accent (00-) and the Lantra's successor, the **Elantra** (01-) are big improvements on their predecessors and have the hallmarks of being decent buys when back on the secondhand market.

The **Coupe** (95, facelift 99, new Dec 01) is a luscious looking sports car. Hugely popular for its styling and keen pricing. The same should apply secondhand. Good buy.

The **Sonata** (96, new 98, big revamp 01) was another value-for-money small-executive buy. Improved a number of times over the years. Well worth a look. Should be good value. Best to buy from 98.

The **Matrix** (late 01-) is a small-compact MPV with a lot of equipment and good pricing. Smallish cabin but an economy buy prospect as a three-year-old.

The roomy **Trajet** MPV (00 - ) also has the hallmarks of a decent purchase. It has been a best seller in its mid-size segment and there are a few on the used market now. As with all MPVs, check for internal wear/use as a taxi.

The **Santa Fe** (Dec 00-) is a typical modern sports utility with a mix of curve and muscle. Good diesels. Popular buy as new and well priced.
The **Terracan** (02- ) is a large SUV aimed at the mainstream 4x4 market. It's big, bland and well priced but there's a lot of competition from traditional 4x4 big names. Price is a plus.

**Jaguar**

Here's a good example of a company improved beyond all recognition. One side-effect of being taken over by Ford is that older Jags live in the shadow of better quality newcomers. From mid-nineties onwards, the quality picks up rapidly. The **XJ** (Sept 94, revised Sep 97, new Feb 03) and **XJ8**, **XJR** and Sovereign edition (98) reflect this steady improvement.

More recent additions such as the new mid-sized executive **S-TYPE** (April 99 -, revamp 02) and the new smaller **X-TYPE** (June 01, addition of 2.0V6 in 02) mean there's the prospect of a decent choice of stylish, well-made Jags on the secondhand market. Well-priced new and good buys secondhand.

The **XK8** (Sep 96, revised Sep 02) is a powerful large executive coupe. Some think it looks as fresh as ever, I think it looks dated. But it is a great performance car - especially with new engines added in 02.

**Kia**

Do NOT buy any model introduced here before 2001. They are old and dated. They were meant to be basement bargains, but they never had the newness of product to make any sort of impact. The new range under a new distributor is better, far more modern and stylish.
It remains to be seen how the latest model lineup, introduced here in 01, cope on the secondhand market.
Price and equipment are the main attractions with the **Rio** small hatchback, **Mentor** saloon, **Shuma** 5dr, **Carens** mid-size MPV, **Sedona** (large MPV) and **Magentis** (executive) facing the tough, longterm task of convincing dealers and buyers of their residual worth in the market place.

**Land Rover**

Also owned by Ford, the quality improvements have kicked in big time.

The **Freelander** (98-) has been a runaway success but earlier models were overshadowed by subsequent revision (late 99, for 00 market). Go for the latter.

The **Discovery** (98 -, with TD5 engine, revised 00, revised 02) has plenty of room and great off-road ability. Earlier models were not nearly as refined as newer versions. But the 02 revision produced the biggest impact on quietness in cabin and handling to date. Puts all predecessors in the shade. Pay used prices accordingly.

The **Range Rover** (95-, old model remained as 'Classic, new model revised 00, new 02- ) is, for many, the ultimate off/on-road luxury machine. Ample room to travel in style and fabulous ability off-road. Older version (pre-02) had fine turbodiesel. Petrols are large and thirsty. New model a big improvement on previous one, so maybe there's a bargain to be had.

The **Defender** (-02, several updates and revisions since 95, including 00) is the great old workhorse of 4x4s. Passenger versions are now sought after for their historic individuality. Diesels best.

**Lexus**

This is Toyota's prestige marque. It has done particularly well since it began selling here in 1990.

Its volume seller is the **IS** range (99 - minor revision 02). The vast majority are 2-litre IS200s. The range got a small facelift, equipment upgrade and a new wagon, the **SportCross** (3-litre) for 02 sale. The 2-litre engine added to the SportCross (Oct 02) makes it a first-class package. The IS200s are justifiably well regarded on the used market. Good buys.

The mid-size sporty coupe **GS** range (93-, big revision late 97; further update, 4.3-litre late 00) tend to hold values better than most in the used car market. Best buys are from 1997 onwards.

Residuals for the larger executive **LS400** (95-00) were always above average despite accusations of being bland. Expect the same for its much better looking successor, the **LS430** (00- ). Exceptional cars that are made to last.

The **RX300** (00-) is an example of the new executive Sports Activity Vehicle (See Chapter 12)  though the automatic gearbox is a tad slow to respond. These are popular in their niche and should be worthwile secondhand prospects.

The **SC430** is a large luxury roadster (01-, suspension changed 03) with all the creature comforts, but the suspension set up and runflat tyres did not suit Irish roads. The company offered to replace existing suspensions for those so wished. From 03 all SC430s have the new setup and they're much better for it.

## Mazda

Always popular second-hand, Mazdas tend to age well and give lots of service. They have added a number of new niche models in recent years. And there's plenty more to come.

The supermini **121** (up to 96) was a quirky looking car with a half-moon profile. You liked or hated it. The subsequent 121 (96, facelift 01, new 03) was a much different shape - a Ford Fiesta in Mazda clothing - with the bonus of a three-year warranty. The newer the better - they're sound buys.

The **323** range comprised some lovely cars up to 1997. There are new, less salubrious looking, models from 1998 (revision 00, new '3' in 04). The 323 is always popular second-hand. It has hatch and saloon (very large interior) body styles and a good range of engines. Does not sparkle as new but fares well on the secondhand market. The big 00 revamp improved the range considerably.

The **626** (-96, new Aug 97, revamp 99, replaced 02) is a popular family/fleet model with a strong range of standard equipment and good build. The older 626 (pre-97) was better looking but the subsequent model had improved handling and ride. Bargain hard for good value here because there are quite a few on the market. The new **Mazda6** (02-) overshadows them on looks, handling and space.

The **Demio** (98 -,1.5-litre added 00, replaced by Mazda2 in 03) is a tidy Midi-MPV-type 5dr which would suit buyers looking for a city/town runaround. Competent and understated. Nice little buy.

The mid-size **Premacy** (99- ) people carrier is a decent buy in its sector, though not as well known as its rivals. Seven seater version (-03) much more competitive on space. Price previous accordingly.

The **Mazda MPV** (00 -, revised, new diesel end 02 for 03) is a large people carrier which has not set the world alight. As an unfussy, roomy vehicle it is a good buy. Bargain hard here.
The **MX-5** (new bodystyle 97 end of pop-up headlights, small revision 99) remains a firm favourite and an excellent small sportscar buy. In good demand despite its length of time on the market.

The **Tribute** is a medium-to-large Sports Utility (June 01-) with both two and four-wheel-drive options. Lot of equipment. Too early for a secondhand track record.

**Mazda Xedos**

Mazda's medium sized executive model is called the **Xedos 9** (94, major revamp Jan 01). Older versions of the smaller **Xedos 6** (-end 99) never caught on and the price you pay should reflect this. The Xedos 9 is a good car, roomy and well equipped. But it is a prime example of second-hand buyers benefiting from cut-throat competition in, and perceptions of, the executive car market. It should be on a bargain hunter's list as depreciation levels from new can be severe.

**Mercedes-Benz**

The marque has broadened its model range significantly over the past few years: from the small MPV A-Class to the large S-600. Huge range of models and engines with the three-pointed star.

The initial **A-Class** (99- big revamp 01 with long wheelbase versions added) was disappointing partly because the materials used in the interior gave it a down-market feel. It also had to contend with a so-called 'roll-over' test failure controversy in its initial stages. This was more imagined than real but didn't do it any good. The 01 revamp made it a far better small Merc but failed to ease the harsh suspension and damper settings. These marked part of the the company's response to the roll-over controversy by ensuring it had less bodyroll than nearly any car on the market. Push very hard for value on pre-2001 versions.

The previous **C-Class** (Sept 93-99) was one of the best-priced small executive motors in its class and consistently added equipment over the years, so the later in the nineties the better in terms of what you get for your money. Good buy.
  The brand new car (99-, new Twinpulse engines Feb 03) is miles ahead on looks and driving but rear seat room and accessibility are by no means class leading. Nice looking coupe version but gearchange is poor.

The **E-Class** (95-, several revisions including 99, engines updated and new diesels) is a great, big car with lots of room. Distinguished from its predecessor by elliptical double-light design at the front. Several revamps over the years and lots of equipment added. The newer the better in terms of overall value: revamp price rises were proportionately lower than the cost of the additions. Good buy.

The arrival of the brand new model (July 02) will help buyers get better deals on older ones. But don't expect too much.

The old **S-Class** (up to 99) was over-priced (25% more than previous model) and oversized. Tell that to any vendor and resist the temptation to plump for the big-car-for-the-money selling line. Its successor (99-, revised 03) is immeasurably better in all departments. You can get a really good deal on an old one now. Big revamp of new S-Class in 2003 will help your bargaining on all fronts.

The **CLK** (97-02, new May 02) is a mix of coupe/roadster/sporty driving and reasonable interior room. Arrival of 02 new model a help if you're buying used predecessor.

The **SLK** (98, minor revisions early 01) is a sharply profiled super car and a three-year-old could be your best buy here.

The **CL** (new 00-, revised 03) has really caught the imagination - in complete contrast to the old one which never caught on. The latter may be to your distinct financial advantage.

The **SL** sports car (-01, new Mar 02) also competes in the rarefied atmosphere of six figure sums. Extremely popular, and previous versions are prized on the secondhand market - ultimate status symbols for those who can, and cannot, afford.

The **M-Class** (late 98/effectively for 99 sale, major revamp early 01) was the first of the executive sports utilities. The extensive 01 revision enhanced it greatly so hit the bargaining buttons if buying models sold before that.

The **V-Class** (97 -, revised Mar 02, new 03) is a large MPV based on a van and driving dynamics can reflect this. But it is enormously roomy and packed with comfort features. Could be a good buy for a larger family as a three-year-old. Try the diesel.

**Mitsubishi**

There haven't been too many outstanding additions to the range over the last few years. They are well-made vehicles and you can benefit from their lack of new-car profile up to 2002.

The large supermini/small-family hatch **Colt** (96-, revised 98) has been around for a long time. It's an attractive little car with plenty of buzz but getting seriously dated. Not bad for a first-car buyer, but bargain hard. Buy 98+ versions.

The small-family **Lancer** (96 - withdrawn 01) was bland but capable. Use knowledge of withdrawal to get a better price on a used one. It's a good, unspectacular, practical buy so long as the price is right. New one late 03.

The **Spacestar** (98-, diesel from 00, revised Sep 02) is a small people carrier that appears to have met a market need for a cross between an MPV and family estate. Tidy and useful, it's a good secondhand buy for its handiness. 02 revamp makes a big difference. Unusually, and best of all, there was no price rise. So maybe you'd be better to buy new.

The **Carisma** (96-, diesels added 96, 00, 1.3-litre from late 01) is a family-fleet car that hides its credentials under a bland exterior. But it is well made, now has a good spread of engines, and should make a particularly good secondhand buy - simply because it is unspectacular.

The executive **Galant** (93, new 97) is a good-value investment: unspectacular to look at but engineered and built to high standard. As a three-to-six-year-old you will benefit from someone else's depreciation but still have a fine motor for years.

The **Spacewagon** (-99, new 99-, new 2-litre Aug 00) has a good name and usually in keen demand on the used-car market. The 1999+ version is larger and more expensive. If buying a pre-99 model, bargain hard. These are good cars and last the pace. However, the new car only had 2.4-litre engines at 99 launch. Go for the subsequent 2-litre - it's more economical. Good buy.

The large SUV/4x4 **Pajero** (-00, new Apr 00, revised Apr 02) has a big reputation. There is a fair choice of passenger and commercial versions with both long and short wheelbases. And there's a Pajero Sport edition. The Pajero is widely regarded as an excellent piece of engineering. A good used buy. There is also a 'mini' specially-styled small version called the **Pinin** (99, 5dr added 02). The 5dr is the only option as far as I'm concerned; 3dr access is really poor.

**Nissan**

A good range to choose from secondhand. The supermini **Micra** (93-02, several revisions, new car 03) is one of the great little cars on the second-hand market. Sound buys, usually well priced and plenty on market - just look at the number in the small ads. Knowing there's a new one from 03 should be useful in whittling down the asking price of an older one.

The **Almera** (95-00; new model 00, revised 03) is a thoroughly competent small-family/medium family car. It is a first class second-hand buy as older versions (before the 2000 new model came along) were seen as dull but well made. Don't mind that. Newer models are better looking and equipped. Practical buys.

The **Primera** (96, upgrade Oct 98 for 99 market, new 02) has been a family/fleet champion for years. Good driving characteristics. Have a look at 1.6-litre petrol versions as they are more likely to have been privately owned than out on car fleets. The spring 2002 arrival of a radically new model puts older versions in the shade - so bargain hard.

The **Tino** (01, revised early 02 with price drop) is Nissan's mid-size MPV. One of the few cars to have added equipment and dropped its price within a year of initial launch. That's good news for anyone wishing to buy secondhand: earlier versions will have come down in re-sale value proportionate to the drop in the new-car price. Your bonus.

The executive **Maxima** (95-, facelift 98, new 00) has a good reputation for comfort and space. Versions of the first series, replaced by a bigger, better model in 2000 are on the market. Go for the 2-litre engine, you don't need the 3-litre. A well-minded model could leave you with a really good, and low-cost, big car for years.

The **Terrano** (93-99, new look/revision 99, minor facelift July 02) is a mid-range 4x4 built as a joint venture with Ford (its version was called the Maverick). Popular enough as a passenger sports utility. Buy as new as possible.
The large 4x4 **Patrol** (Dec 97, replaced Apr 00 and new 3-litre engine) is highly rated but used versions of new model unlikely to be numerous. Genuinely impressive on the road. Sound buy.

The **X-Trail** (02-) is one of the smoothest sports utilities on the road. New to market in 02, it will be a good acquisition secondhand. Despite some over-use of plastic in the dash area, it is/will be a quality buy.

The **Serena** (95 - off market 02) MPV is van based and drives as such. Expect low used-car prices. Just don't expect too much. This is motoring at its most basic and practical; there are few frills. Bargain hard and make sure you check it for previous use as a taxi or company workhorse.

The **200SX** (-00) is low-key on looks but can produce high octane performance. Nice, understated, car to own. Prices should be attractive now.

**Opel**

The marque is popular here, so there is always a good volume of secondhands to choose from an extensive dealer network.

The **Agila** (00-) is Opel's mini-MPV. It's tall, angular and roomy inside. The 1-litre 3-cylinder engine has its own distinct sound which may not be everyone's cup of tea. Preference is for the larger 1.2-litre.

The **Corsa** (93-00; new car Oct 00) has had quite a few upgrades over the years. Plentiful on the secondhand market, check if the one you're interested in was used as a hire car for the first six months of its life because they are popular on rental fleets.

The newer **Astra** (90, new 98 -) is noticeably larger than its more compact and rounded predecessor. It should be a better buy for that, though it is more expensive. Solid cars. Plenty on the market. Compare prices from a number of garages.

The **Vectra** (96, facelift 99, new 02) is a tale of two halves. The old one (96-02) was not much to look at and was outshone in several departments by many rivals. The new one is a lot larger, smarter and better in every department. Use that to significantly improve your bargaining position on buying an older one.

The **Tigra** was a cute little two-seater (95-00) that made small 'sports car' driving affordable for hundreds of buyers. It has dated and should be a good-money buy now.

The **Zafira** (99-, facelift 03) is one of the marque's true success stories. It is a larger mid-size MPV with three rows of seats – the third row folds flat into the floor to provide exceptional space.

Well worth a look secondhand provided you're satisfied it hasn't been hacked by previous occupants. First class buy but secondhand asking prices can be stiff.

Opel had a large MPV, the **Sintra**, here for a couple of years (97 - discontinued 99). There are few of them about. The mere fact they discontinued it should give you bargaining leverage. Buy at rock bottom money.

The **Omega** (94, revised 00) replaced in 03 by **Signum** is Opel's flagship. You should be able to sniff out a good bargain on a three or four-year-old because it too lacks 'snob' value in the executive market. Turbodiesels excellent. Productive territory for the budget conscious buyer, especially if you get an estate.

The **Frontera** (-95 -, several revisions) is a mid-sized SUV which has always been one of the better drivers on the road. The cabin and instrumentation were terribly old fashioned in its earlier days but modernisation has muted their detractions. Buy from latter years.

The **Calibra** (-97) was a fine sports car but out of the frame for some time now. At the right money an attractive driver but age and fresher rivals are heavily against it. Watch for heavy use.

The **Speedster** (01-) is an outrageously designed two-seater sports car with dramatic performance. Scarcity should help secondhand values.

**Peugeot**

Traditionally popular in rural areas for its diesels, it now has a stylish, more modern range aimed at younger, urban buyers as well. Some innovative new models have caught the imagination.

The **106** (92 -, revised 96 -) is a small car with pace and poise and there are several versions to choose from. Good little driver and handy around town. Dated but a decent buy.
The **205** (- 97) overshadowed subsequent Peugeots for a long time because it was such a driver's car. Hard to get one within our buying-time frame now.

The **206** (98 -, slight revisions 03) is the 205's natural successor. It has style and good room. There was a noticeable difference in the early models because entry-level 206 1.1-litre L versions did not have anti-roll bars. It showed in the handling.

Roll bars were fitted at the end of 2000. So check. Highly popular from new, there should be quite a few coming on the used market at affordable rates.

The **306** (95-97; big upgrade 97, finished 01) was among the best handling small-family cars of its generation. Now overtaken by its successor, the 307 (01) it should be available at reasonable money now.

The **307** (01-) is a European Car of the Year winner and is substantially larger than the 306. Lacks the vivacity of the 306 but is a better all-round small-family package. Few on the secondhand market as yet.

The family fleet **405** (-95) is really dated now. Lot of extra equipment in later models. Diesels best.

Its successor, the **406** (96, revised 99, new model 04) is far superior and has picked up several awards. Lot of room, equipment and special driving feel. You'll buy this at good money on the secondhand market. Coupe versions (97-, 2.2-litre petrol late 02) and estates are well worth a look. Fine diesels.

The marque never made a big market impression with its executive models. Used prices for the **605** (- 98) plummeted – an opportunity to buy a big car for small money.

Its successor, the **607** (01-) has fared better, though the heavy level of depreciation among less traditional executive marques will please the bargain hunters.

The **806** (94-01) people carrier (a Peugeot badged version of the Citroen Synergie and Fiat Ulysse) wasn't much of a seller and is an okay used-car buy at the right price only. Check for wear and tear. New car, the **807,** early 03.

**Porsche**

Buyers of these pricey sports cars know more about them than most others in the marketplace. Exterior and interior condition, detailed service records, mileage and previous ownership are critical in performance cars. If you are thinking of buying a **911** Carrera (98-), go for a later nineties model for much better handling. Great to drive, exceptional pace and good variety.

The **Boxster** (97-) was introduced here to much acclaim. Dynamic looking, a great drive and a marvellous cabin. Could be a really good secondhand buy as Porsche owners tend to treat their motors exceptionally well.

## Renault

The old **Clio** (up to 98) was a spirited little car and still worth considering. The new one (98-, substantial revamp Jul 01) is distinguished by its curved rear window and the introduction of a 1.2-litre engine. Also well worth looking at. These tend to stick around for a long time. Value buys. Revised version (01-) much better.

The **Megane** (96 -, revamp in 99, radical new car, late 02) stretches from hatchback to saloon (very roomy) to smart-looking Coupe and original mid-size people carrier, the Scenic. Good cars in their day but the radical nature of their late 02 successor emphasises the time gap between new and old. Use to your secondhand buying advantage.

The **Scenic** (97-, 01 revision, 1.4-litre added, new car 03) is an undoubted good buy, new or used, if you're looking for a compact people/small-family carrier. Before they added a 1.4-litre, the entry level engine was a 1.6-litre. Benchmark car and well worth a look.

The old **Laguna** (94-, revamp 96) was a roomy, well equipped family/fleet car. It should be good value on the secondhand market now its awarding winning same-name successor (01-) has taken over. Innovative new one is strong on style, space, safety and equipment.

Here's where you'll get exceptional value on the used-car market. The executive **Safranc** (93-00, with revisions) was ultimately replaced by the radically different, and excellent, **Vel Satis** (02). But it suffered heavy depreciation due to poor market perception i.e. no 'snob' value. Comfortable and roomy. Better engines later in life. Small money gets you big car or you don't buy.
The large people carrier **Espace** is one of the class leaders (-97; 97-02, revised 00, brand new car 03). Spacious and versatile, it is likely to be good value as a three or four-year-old. There is a good turbodiesel version.

Finally, there is the unusual looking **Kangoo Kar** (00-02 ), an ultra-practical, small people carrier/van based vehicle. Good value new and likely to be even better value secondhand.

## MG Rover

As Rover, they were devastated when former owner BMW pulled out. It meant the range was under-funded and left behind by most other manufacturers. The new company, MG Rover, has performed miracles to upgrade and modernise models (from late 2001) but the range is still largely based on rapidly dating originals.

Avoid Rover **100s** or **200s** (214s, 216s etc,) up to 1999 despite tempting prices. They are outdated and there are several better small-car options.

The Rover **25** (99 - ) is an 'in-between' car (supermini and small-family) which never really caught on. Underrated car and prices may be tempting but long term residuals need to be considered.

The **400** series (revised 95, - 99) was a decent car in its time (5dr smaller than 4-dr saloon) but the subsequent upgraded **45** (99 -) is a better proposition and, though still dated, is likely to be better value for money.

Before troubled times hit Rover, the large family/small executive **600** series (93-99) was the best of the model range. There are a number on the secondhand market but they are starting to date now. 623i was best but 1.8-litre 618i, in particular, still worth a look at the right money.

Its successor, the **75** (99-, estate 01), is a larger, more expensive, upmarket model but of sufficient durability to be marked out as a 3/4/5-year-old buying opportunity. They positioned it to fill the void left by departure of the **800** series (86-99, several revisions) which should be avoided unless it has truly exceptional low mileage (unlikely) and pricing (likely).

Older Rover models will pale rapidly with the advent of the MG derivatives (from late 01) **ZR, ZS** and **ZT** which differ substantially in terms of performance and have much better road presence.

## MGF

The **MGF** convertible (95-, revisions 99) was good to look at but only moderate in every other respect. Not a patch on Mazda MX-5 for example. Replaced by **MGTF** in March 2002.

**Saab**

Owned by General Motors (Opel), Saab has been left alone to focus on its traditional strongholds of safety and engine development. This comes across more and more with every new model.

The old **900** (78-98, several revisions) had a loyal following, which continued when renamed the **9-3** (from 98, diesel added Oct 98). Convertible versions very popular.

A vastly improved all-new **9-3 Sport Saloon** (Sept 02) marks the beginning of a new family of Saabs, but earlier **9-3s** remain popular as secondhands with a devoted coterie of buyers.

The **9000** (94-97) was a great driving car of its era. There are good, if limited, examples around but they should be well priced. Just getting a bit old now for our timeframe.

The larger executive **9-5** (97-, estate 99, diesels added Aug 01 and 02, major revamp Sep 01) is exceptionally strong on safety. Again, the big 02 revision puts previous models at a disadvantage - and you at an advantage if you're looking for one.

**Seat**

This marque has been steadily on the rise since the early nineties. New models have put a lot of emphasis on style and the diesels are excellent. Seat is owned by Volkswagen and it shows in the quality of the cars produced. Sturdy and durable buys.

The **Arosa** (97-01) was an excellent value-for-money city car. Its successor (early 02) is far too expensive. Older versions are therefore likely to be much better value. Good first-buy secondhand cars.

**Ibiza** superminis (93-, revamps 96, 99, new spring 02) are solid buys generally. Go for later-in-nineties versions which benefitted from big improvements, including an impressive new look.
Avoid earlier models without power steering. Good buys.
The **Cordoba** (93– , revamp 99; brand new 03) is generally regarded as an Ibiza with a boot though the makers say it is more than that. This is popular for its style and compact handiness. Well priced new; good value second-hand.

The **Leon** (00- ) is a much-fancied small-family/sport hatch, which has the hallmarks of a good buy as a three or four year old.

The old **Toledo** (91-99) was a great stalwart. It was at its best late in life and had a bargain basement price. The new one (99 -) is more compact, stylish and, ultimately, totally different. It has fine diesel engines. Old one for real value; new one for style.

The **Alhambra** MPV (96 - 00; big revamp late 00 for 01) is closely related (another joint venture) to the Ford Galaxy and VW Sharan but has been better priced. Big revamp worked wonders for it - but maybe not for predecessor's values. You benefit.

**Skoda**

Now very much a household name with a good recent pedigree – it too is owned by Volkswagen. Try not to buy anything before 1997 though prices can tempt. Later versions of the 'old regime' **Felicia** (95-00, revised 98) hatch and estate were not bad at all and represented great value-for-money. But their roots lie in an era when Skoda was only starting its turnaround. You're better off buying cars that made that transformation.

Look seriously at the large-supermini **Fabia** models (00-, 1.2-litre added 02) on the used market. This is sturdy, stylish and roomy (especially saloons). Good buy.

The same goes for the family 5dr hatch **Octavia** (98 -, revamp 00). Older versions were a bit cramped in the rear but still good value. Economical 1.4-litre version introduced with late 2000 revamp which also added more rear-seat space. Fine buy new/secondhand. Good diesels too. Popular now as taxis, so check history.

The **Superb** (02-) is a large executive which competes on price, equipment and space. Too soon to make predictions on used values but the prognosis is good.

**Subaru**

A niche producer of cars engineered to a high standard - as performances of its cars in the world rally championships clearly show. Subaru has a long tradition of making all-wheel-drive models.
These give extra traction and added sure-footedness. If you live in areas exposed to frosty or slippery conditions this can be an added bonus. But a small dealer network militates against wider recognition. A pity. They've some good cars.

The **Vivio** (93-, upgrades to 99) is not a shining example, however. It's an old and a dated city car now and well outstripped by rivals.

The **Justy** (97-01,various upgrades) also has little to offer on the used market that its many supermini rivals don't have in abundance.

The **Impreza** (92-, WRX 00, new 02) is a performance oriented small-family motor. Energetic driving appeal is a main attraction here if you're going after a three or four-year-old. High-performance WRX (00 for 01) is a road-going version of the rally car. Watch for signs of over-zealous driving.

The **Legacy** (94-, new 00) is an accomplished, but underrated, large family/executive car. You will find a few good examples - as well as some fine versions of the **Outback** derivative - on the used market. Worth considering especially if there's a Subaru dealer nearby.

The **Forester** (97-, revised 99, new Jan 03) is a mix between an estate and a sports utility. Nice, clean driver with first rate engineering and build. Not trendy looking, underrated but a fine vehicle. Good secondhand buy.

**Suzuki**

Well-known maker of small cars, it has broadened its range in recent times.

Early **Altos** (95 -, new generation 02) and **Swifts** (- 97, new generation 97-01, new model 01) have slipped behind their competitors in terms of dynamics and modernity. New Alto (02-) a big improvement visually. Some well-priced secondhands but you're much better off buying new.

The **Wagon R** (98 -, became Wagon R+ in 00 revision) is unusual. Short, tall and angular with lots of cabin room, it shares the same base as the Opel Agila. Owning such an unusual looking motor is a matter of taste. But a practical buy.

The **Ignis** (01 -) is a modern well-priced and equipped supermini. Surprisingly energetic to drive. Should be good used option.

The **Baleno** (95 -, several upgrades, off market 02) is an understated small-family car. It was keenly priced new and secondhand values reflect this. Unfussy, practical buy.

The **Liana** (5dr, 01 -, 4dr 02) is a mix of supermini, small-family hatch and small-MPV. Tall and roomy, it should make a straightforward, if unspectacular, three-year-old purchase.

The little 4-wheel-drive **Jimny** (98, revised 00) is popular with female drivers and younger buyers. Mix of urban runaround and small, tough off-road competitor. Interesting purchase secondhand - at the right money.

The larger **Vitara** was around a long time, but stood the test well and is popular secondhand. The **Grand Vitara** (98-) sports utility is highly competent. Emphasis on car-like qualities. Cabin on the tidy side but a good buy new/used.

## Toyota

Has expanded and upgraded its range substantially since 2000. Renowned for the reliability of its products, it consistently comes at, or near, the top of owner satisfaction ratings worldwide. Secondhand values among the best as a result.

The **Starlet** (- 99), although superseded by the award winning Yaris (99-), remains a second-hand favourite. The nearer to 1999 the better.

Its successor, the **Yaris** (99-), is a compact supermini with design flair. Hugely popular, it's a good used buy as its value will hold better than class average. Also a mini-MPV **Verso** version (Dec 99 -) but it's expensive.

The **Corolla** (- 97; new 97-01; brand new car 01-) is synonymous with reliability and has a rock solid re-sale reputation. Four-door saloons (97-01) are top used choices. Estate versions of pre-01 car look well. There's an MPV-type Corolla **Verso** as well (01-) but it is expensive.

The **Carina E** (-97) was always among the roomiest of family/fleet cars but later models were far superior.

Its successor the **Avensis** (97 for 98; new VVT-i engines, D4D diesel, facelift late 00, brand new car 03) improved substantially over the years too, especially with arrival of new hi-tech VVT-I engines from late 2000. These made a big difference.

An opportunity to bargain harder on earlier models. Remarkable 2-litre D4D diesel well worth a look for big mileage drivers.

The executive **Camry** (buy older model from late 1996, effectively 97; brand new car late 01 -) is a top-class secondhand buy. Exceptionally well built. Has not been regarded as premier league executive player though mechanical pedigree suggests it should be otherwise. Secondhand values disproportionately low when quality is taken into account. Good buy in anyone's books.

The mid-size people carrier **Picnic** (Nov 96-00) appealed on its good mix of space and price. It's deceptively roomy. Nice buy.

It was replaced by the **Avensis Verso** (01-) which is particularly roomy and, with Toyota's name, will be a longterm good buy on the secondhand market.

The sports utility **RAV4** (-00, new Sep 00-) is also well worth a look as a used SUV. Popular as new, it is understandably in demand on the secondhand market. Mostly a style statement on the tarmac but they have top-rate 4x4 engineering.

The large 4x4 **Land Cruiser** (Oct 96 - revised 00 with new D4D engine; new Dec 02) is an immensely powerful modern SUV/4x4. Well equipped, it is made to go on and on.

The **Prius** (00 for 01-) is a hybrid electric-petrol car that appeals environmentally but the price is steep despite a VRT concession by the Government. Mostly a corporate purchase.

The sharply defined **Celica** sports car (95/6 – 99; Mar 00, revised late 02 for 03) is an eyecatcher. Newer versions (00-) are better due to improved handling and engine technology. If buying older models bargain hard on that basis.

The **MR2** (-00, new Mar 00 -, revised 03) is a mid-engined high-performance sports car with serious driving ability. Always a demand for cars like this - at the right price.

The **Previa** (-01; brand new 01 -) is a large MPV with lots of room and equipment. New car is light years ahead of old one and has a fine diesel, so bargain for the latter - and check for wear.

## Volkswagen

Has built a big reputation for the durability and build quality of its cars, a fact reflected in the level of new and secondhand values.

The city car **Lupo** (99 -) is solid and robust. Go for the 1-litre (999cc) version. These have high residual values and stand accused of being overpriced when new. GTi version a cracker. Fine used buy.

The supermini **Polo** (95-01, new one early 02) is something of a classic but be careful. It only got power steering on all models quite late in its previous existence. What looks like a good deal on an earlier model may not have this critical element. Check because its absence won't be highlighted. If it hasn't, you will miss it badly. Excellent saloon versions as well. Good all-round reputation. New one continues with tradition.

The **Golf** (-97, new 98, new 03-) is a renowned used-car buy. The old shape gave way to the new in 1998 yet used values don't reflect this as much as it would with some other marques. Expect longevity not short term bargains from secondhand Golfs.

The old Golf's saloon counterpart was the **Vento** (92-98) a spacious workhorse. Dated now, it might still be worth a look - if you want a roomy, economical (especially diesel) motor.

The **Bora** (98 -, revisions, engines added 00) is VW's mid-size saloon. Underrated for driving, and pricey. Typical Volkswagen package of sturdiness and solidity. Undoubtedly good secondhand buy but watch the price.

The large family-fleet **Passat** (96-, big revamp late 00) has been used as the benchmark against which other marques compare. Holds value well, bargains hard come by. Diesels good, smaller petrols fine for family use.

Hard to gauge how the new **Beetle** (00-) will fare on the used market longterm. Lovely to look at and drive but very cramped in the rear seats.

If you can get your hands on a well-minded **Sharan** people carrier (96 -, revision late 00) with a 1.9Tdi engine, you should give it some thought. Make sure it wasn't used as a taxi. Clean, straight four-year-old is a good buy.

## Volvo

Owned by Ford, the marque has expanded and significantly improved its range. Renowned for safety and quality of build.

Four and five-year-old versions of the small executive **S40** (saloon) and **V40** (estates) are good value on the used-car market. These (96-, several upgrades) are well equipped, comfortable and better drivers than they're credited with being. Long term good buys. Use improvements in later models to strengthen your buying hand if considering older versions.

The S40/V40 were preceded by the **440/460** ranges (- 97). In their later years these had a lot of equipment, but as add-ons mean little financially at this stage of their lives, you should battle extremely hard on price.

The **S60** (00 for 01-) is a sporty/saloon which has impressed with power and handling. Nice buy.

The **850** (-97) was a breakthrough car for Volvo; it had power, pace and panache. But it is now dated. So bargain hard on price. Estate versions were exceptional. Expect real value at this stage.

The 850 was effectively replaced by, and renamed, the **S70/V70** saloon-estate (97 -, some revisions and major engine additions over the years).

A brand new **V70,** based on the platform of the larger luxury S80 platform arrived in 2000. Great estate, and fine secondhand buy.

The **S80** (98 -, engine additions include new diesel 01) is a big, hugely comfortable executive car, but let down by its handling and ride. Use that to get a better price secondhand.

The **C70 Coupe** (96- ) is a large coupe but not overly impressive on the road. Nice enough buy at the right money.
And finally, the old **940** (-97) and **960** (-95, subsequently badged **S90** saloon and **V90** estate (-98) large car partnership was so well equipped, so hard on fuel and now so outdated, they will make someone a really solid secondhand buy if they don't mind the heavy petrol bills. Work hard on price. These go forever.

## Section II

## Chapter 15

# Paying for it

Finding the car is one thing. Finding the money to buy it is another. Most of us have to borrow. And just as with the search for a car, the ads can be our starting point.

There are strict rules on how car finance deals are advertised. Advertisers must spell out the nature and details of the finance deal they're offering.

For example the total higher purchase price should be clear. In the case of consumer hire (lease) agreements, it also has to be clearly stated that the car belongs to the lease company.

**Licence to loan**

All garages/dealers that arrange loans are required to hold an authorisation certificate issued by the Director of Consumer Affairs. This must be on public display.

They also must give a written quotation detailing the exact nature of the financial package. Don't sign anything until you get this.

There are a myriad of finance deals on the market, all offering 'unbeatable' value.

**Remember!** you are buying two products - the car and the

finance package. However, the car will depreciate but the finance package won't.
Always bear in mind that dealers and salespeople get big incentives to arrange your finance.

**Money for hire**

You can finance your car purchase in any of the following ways.
- a personal loan. Usually the best deal if you can get it.
- a term loan. Fixed rate, fixed term. You have to state the purpose of the loan.
- a credit union loan. Can also be competitive.
With these loans you own the car immediately.
You just owe the money to an institution.

**The write stuff**

Under the Consumer Credit Act 1995, the nature of any credit agreement has to be clearly stated. That is so you know, for example, that it is a 'hire purchase', a 'credit/sale' agreement or a 'consumer hire' deal.
You must get a copy of the agreement within ten days of making it. If you don't, it may be legally unenforcable.
In addition it must have a breakdown of all the financial commitments - and outline the penalties on default.
Again if any of these are missing, the agreement may be unenforcable.

**Two-in-one**

Hire purchase - in its many guises - is the most popular form of financing a car.
The hire purchase (HP) price includes the deposit, repayments, documentation fees and all other charges connected with the agreement.
In reality a HP deal is two agreements in one
1. You agree to 'rent' the car.
2 And to purchase it at the end of the agreement (*you can also buy the car during the course of the agreement if you wish to*).

Don't forget you have certain rights under a HP agreement.
For example if you have paid one-third of the hire purchase price the finance house may have to go to court if it wishes to terminate the agreement.
If you have half the HP price paid, you can terminate the deal giving notice in writing that you intend to do so.
But remember under a hire purchase deal you DO NOT own the car until the last repayment has been made, or you buy the car outright.

**Never yours**	In a consumer hire agreement (leasing), you never own the car. If you default, you are tied into the full amount. These are regarded as bad value for private buyers but make sense for companies as they can claim back VAT and depreciation against tax.

**Balloon payments**	A balloon payment is a final lump sum owed at the end of the repayment period. It is calculated on the expected value of the car (usually) as a three-year-old.
Those offering such packages insist they err on the side of caution in doing their sums. That's so the residual value of the car will more than cover the lump sum payment owed - and leave you with money towards your next car.
Unfortunately, that is not always the case, especially where a model's secondhand values have plummeted. And few escaped the heavy falls in values in 2001. As a result, some people have found, to their utter dismay, that the value of the car is substantially less than the amount still owing on it.
Nowadays, you will find these balloon payments only in hire purchase agreements.
And remember that your rights may be diluted with these as it will take longer to reach the critical one-third and one-half stages of paying the HP price which give you certain rights.

TIP! Dealers and finance house dress up different deals under diiferent names - from personal contract purchase to personal ownership finance deals - but don't forget they are basically all hire purchase.

**Full price**	Above everything else, check if the deal involves paying the full selling price (no discount) of the car.
If it does, you may be paying substantially more for the vehicle than if its sale was not linked to a finance deal and you could buy 'straight'.
You may well find you are paying interest on the discount you did not get. The difference in interest alone on a €15,000 price instead of a discounted €14,000 adds €150 more at 5% and €240 more at 8% over the total three-year repayment period. That's the road tax on some cars for a year. Worth remembering. If only to improve your chances of getting a better finance deal.

**Small money, big losses**	It is easy to lose sight of even bigger losses in financing a car. A difference of €10-a-week comes to around €1,550 over three years. At €20-a-week the figure soars to over €3,000.

It is easy not to 'miss' small amounts at the start.
But the extra is coming out of your pocket one way or the other.
To have €10 to dispose of, a person on PAYE has to earn nearly €20-a-week (€1,000 a year) before tax. Over three years that's €3,000 before tax.
Think of all the fuss there would be if a reduction or rise of €40-a-month (€10-a-week) in mortgage repayments was announced.

**TIP!** Work hard to contain costs by making simple calculations on the least expensive way to finance a car.

## Think Total Cost of Credit

Finding the bottom line is the only way to assess the worth of a finance deal.
Add up all the payments from deposit to balloon or final payment, for each of the options on offer.
Ultimately, you are looking for a simple figure: how much is this going to cost in interest and related fees alone over the term of the loan.
The TOTAL COST OF CREDIT should be clearly printed or written out for you. Do not agree to anything until it is, and you have thought about it.
APR (annual percentage rate) applies to credit deals only.
Some of the ads for HP deals state an APR, though it is not a legal requirement. But it can be confusing as it may convey the impression that you own the car. Never forget that you do not own the car under a HP deal until it's fully paid for.
And that you never own the car in a consumer hire deal.

## Can't keep up

Many people have found they just cannot keep up with repayments. That is why it is so important to know the extent of outlay in buying, running and financing a car before you do anything.
If you get into difficulty with repayments, the best advice is to arrange to meet the lender and explain your situation as soon as possible.
Whatever happens, do NOT let it drag on. The Money Advice and Budgeting Services (MABS) is free and confidential. Independent and Government funded, they will work out a budget and negotiate with creditors. *See Appendix*.
Remember if your car is repossessed, you may face severe penalties. For example, a repossessed car is normally sold at public auction.

You are liable for the differences between
a) what they get for it at auction, plus what you've paid, plus a special rebate
and
b) the total HP price.
And that can be substantial.
However, before the agreement is terminated, the finance house must notify you (this is called a Section 54 Notice). If you get this then you know it is a final warning. It gives you 21 days to rectify the situation. If nothing is done, they terminate the agreement and initiate proceedings.
Don't let it get to this. Seek help.

And finally on this topic: consumers have a duty of care. You are liable if you damage a car over and above normal wear and tear.

## Loan insurance

Insurance on finance deals can be expensive and unnecessary. They are only options.
You can be offered any one of three policies.
**1.** Cover for illness and unemployment. There are a lot of exclusions. For example, you are not covered under voluntary redundancy.
**2.** GAP - Guaranteed Asset Protection. If you write off the car, the insurance company will only pay the market value. But this will pay the difference between the market price and the hire purchase price. This is the most valuable of these insurances.
**3.** WAP - Warranty Asset Protection. Supposed to guarantee the car parts. But you should be covered under the Sales of Goods and Supply of Services Act and don't need it. In other words you're paying insurance for rights you already have.

# Chapter 16

# When to hold on and when to let go

Changing a car is a costly business. But there are options which can save you money. Buying well-regarded 3-to-4-year-olds is a definite avenue.

**Case for change**

The argument for changing to a new or newer model every two or three years has its merits - if you can afford to.

It means you have an up-to-date car and a good idea of what the costs will be over a particular period of time.

The early years of ownership are the heaviest for depreciation, so you lose in that regard.

But the advantage is that the cost of change is more likely to be consistent.

Other than regular servicing, there is little prospect of additional costs. Subject to reasonable mileage, changing every two/three years means you are never far from the manufacturer's warranty and you benefit from technological advances.

**Slipping back**

But with young families, and a big mortgage, it can be a financial strain to stick with this timeframe - especially where there are two cars involved.

A new car purchase may have to be postponed for a year or two longer than anticipated. And then it can be a vicious circle with a car drifting quickly in value and opening up a wide gap between it and the price of a new one.

Depending on circumstances, it may helpful when you buy new to set a deadline - be it two, three or four years – to do so again. Regard that not so much as a time by which you have to spend money as to save it.

The reasoning goes as follows:

Your new car drops in value at a certain rate for the first two to three years. Keep it a fourth year and - let's say - it will drop another €1,750.

Factor that into your calculations and the cost of buying new after three years is effectively lowered by €1,750.

In a way you are going to spend that money one way or the other. Either through depreciation - by keeping the car.

Or through spending - by purchasing a new one.
Admittedly, this is all paper-money talk, and no one is advocating expenditure where heavy borrowings or additional hardships are incurred.
But thinking about it, and coming up with a manageable way of dealing with it now, may prevent the accumulation of a few years' depreciation turning into a massive gap between the value of your existing car and a new one.

**Newer is safer**

Finance apart, the compelling reason for changing regularly is safety. The newer the model, the safer it is likely to be. There are big technical advances every year.
And the NCT test puts a heavy emphasis on this area.
Therefore, your 'old' car may incur heavier preparation/repair costs to meet the standards. By changing a little earlier you may save on such expenditure. We'll look at that in detail later.

**Keeping it longer**

Another option is to hold on to the car for as long as possible provided it is not too expensive to maintain roadworthy and safe, then replace with a newer model for relatively small outlay.
This all depends on skillful buying and a bit of luck with repairs. But the NCT car test may impose potentially expensive preparation and you have to weigh that up against perceived savings.

**Danger of drift**

Sometimes the car allowed to 'drift' is the one most frequently used to carry children.
The family car should be kept as the newer of a two-car pool because it is likely to be safer. Just remember: most accidents happen near home on short journeys.

**Test it and see**

If you don't know whether to sell your current car now, or take a chance on testing it, the best advice is: Test it and See.
Basically this allows you to find out what is wrong with it and then get an estimate of the NCT printout result from your garage/mechanic to see how much it will cost to put right.
The cost of testing is relatively small compared with banking on someone finding the problems, and paying for the parts and labour. There's still no guarantee the garage/mechanic will pick up on everything. Far better to let hi-tech equipment at an NCT test centre detect them for you.

**Remember!** you do not have to display a 'failure disc'.

With their results in hand, you know exactly what needs to be done. And you'll see at a glance if it is worthwhile spending money on the required repairs.

If it is, you can go back to the NCT centre with your repaired car, have a re-test and (most likely) pass.

If it's not, you've saved a lot by not engaging a mechanic and paying for parts.

**Is it worth it?**

You also have to ask if spending €500 on an old car just to sell or trade it in, will pay you back.

There is a good chance that, regardless of condition, the dealer who takes it against a newer one, will have difficulty selling it on. Most likely it will be moved out to the trade, or used for parts. This will be factored into what you get for it.

Expect it to cost you as much to change to that newer car whether or not your old trade-in has passed its test.

You could end up losing on the double.

**Holding on, saving money**

That's the downside. But the car in question may be good for several years. If you are satisfied it can safely last the pace without heavy expenditure, you could be better off getting the repairs carried out, re-testing and keeping it.

The reasoning goes like this:

If your car is in good condition and has given little trouble it may be worth more to keep than sell.

If you have just spent €1,000 leaving it fit to pass the test, you are unlikely to recoup your money from the market place. But you may get many multiples of its value by keeping it for another two (next test) or three years.

Even if you get nothing at all for it afterwards, it will have more than repaid your investment. Provided it does not incur further significant repair bills, of course.

After two or three years, you could scrap it, or sell it for parts (for a nominal amount) and purchase a new or newer car with the independence of a buyer unfettered by a trade-in.

Taking this hold-on option could save thousands of euro. You do not have to finance a larger sum to purchase, and depreciation levels on your existing car are already as near to negligible as makes no difference.

But be completely happy you are not compromising safety under any circumstances. If you have any doubts at all, you should seriously consider selling and buying something newer and safer.

**Scrapping**

A car can become a real liability in the latter stages of its life. Disposing of it can be a problem. One option is to scrap it, legally. If you do, you should make sure you get a receipt from the scrapping company. Photocopy it and send it with the Vehicle Licensing Cert to the Vehicle Registration Unit, Shannon Co Clare. The vehicle's registration certificate should be sent to Vehicle Office, Rosslare Harbour, Co Wexford.

But before scrapping, it might be worth your while to check with a local dismantler garage, or parts operator. They may buy it for parts – at least you'll get something for it. (Paperwork explained, Page 132). Often, the sum of an old car's worth is less than the collective value of its individual parts, as you'll discover if you have to buy an item second-hand. But it may be better than being penalised at a dealership for a trade-in that no one wants. Otherwise you can pay to have it crushed.

**If thinking of selling**

Test your car and see. Assess and see whether you would be better off holding, selling separately/privately, scrapping or trading in.

**If thinking of buying**

Avail of the ready-made used-car check list based on the NCT specifications (*outlined in Chapter 20*).

Chapter 17

# Selling second-hand

Given that you may have to sell your own car either as a trade-in or on the open market - before during or after buying - it is useful to know a bit about selling secondhand.

As we know, a trade-in can be a bonus or a millstone. A good car in top condition will always get a good price. A bad one may cost you on the double.

That's why the day you buy is the day you sell. If you buy 'right' you have a better chance of trading right and buying right again. Start thinking about selling, like buying, by checking prices quoted in papers, websites and at dealers to get a fix on a band of prices, an upper and lower level of worth for a car of your make, model and year. You will quickly get an idea of values.

**Devil's advocate**

Try to be your car's devil's advocate.

See what you'd pick out as being wrong with it if it were being offered to you for sale. It's a good way of coming up with a realistic price gauge.

While stressing the good points, be prepared to accept some aspects could be better.

But acknowledge them; don't capitulate.

If your car is in good condition and someone offers less than you estimate it to be worth, then refer them to the going rate in the ads or garages which you have previously checked out.

A below-average offer may also be the only one from a dealer with several similar vehicles lying unsold on the back lot. That's why it is so important to shop around: another dealer may not be as overloaded and have a market for it.

Do not sell a car knowing it to have a serious fault. It could lead to an accident.

## Auctions: selling

An auction can be a clean way of selling your car.

It also gives you a chance to see what it's worth to one set of potential buyers. Pitch its reserve a fair bit below the average prices being quoted in the ads, or have someone in the trade put a ballpark figure on it. If it sells, you have money in your pocket to go and buy 'straight' elsewhere.

If it doesn't, you have a better idea of its worth in one context. Auction prices tend to be a good deal lower than those on the private/trade-in market.

Do not shoot yourself in the foot by asking auction prices if you are selling privately or as a trade-in.

Revert to using the price ranges in the small ads as your starting point.

## Prepared to sell

A car can put off potential buyers, or fail the NCT test, for silly but obvious oversights. Make sure it has adequate oil and water.

Empty out the boot and keep the seats clear of personal belongings.

Give it a good clean all over, especially the underbody.

Make sure the tyres have a good tread depth and are inflated to the correct pressure.

Time the servicing of your car to coincide with the sale or the test.

**Remember!** The biggest first-time failure items are lights not properly focused for full beam or dim, brakes and exhaust emissions.

Attend to these areas. Get the car tuned and ticking over as smoothly as possible. NCT emissions standards for older cars are NOT those applied to current newer models. They are linked to levels determined as reasonable for its age. A good tuning should suffice. The performance of brakes, front, rear and handbrake fail quite a few at test. No matter what, brakes should always be in first-class working order.

# Chapter 18

# And now, the final curtain call

You have made the mental decision to buy.
You are just about to sign on the dotted line.
You have thought about this for a long time.
Now you want to get on with it.
Take one more minute.
Run a mental check on each of the following just to be 100% sure.
Be completely honest.

**Your last-minute 10-point checklist**

1. Is this the car you really wanted and needed when you started out?
2. Would you say it is bigger, smaller, nicer, better value/worse value, than you envisaged when you set out to buy?
3. How often have you changed your mind about the car you need?
4. Have you checked out the reputation of the seller and the car?
5. Are you sure the price is right? Have you shopped around?
6. Did you get quotes for your trade-in and the new/newer car from several dealers?
7. Have you had somebody else assess it with you?
8. Have you considered the finance/running/depreciation costs in detail? Are you sure they are manageable?
9. Is there any little thing that still niggles, or you don't like about the car or the deal?
10. Are you completely happy with the dealer/garage/salesperson?

**How did you fare?**

If you are only 75% positive, you may need to reassess.
If you are 95% + positive, then all the best with your new acquisition.

Section III

Chapter 19

# There may be trouble ahead

It is the nature of a consumer item built on moving parts that faults develop and things go wrong.
Motoring is a difficult area for legislation to comprehensively cover.
It is never easy to be absolutely clearcut about who should do what for whom.
You have legal protection and your consumer rights (outlined over the next few pages) but there are many grey areas.
The legislation under which consumer transactions take place is the Sale of Goods and Supply of Services Act 1980.

**Problem cars**

Many car owners find, after going back and getting 'satisfaction', they still have a problem. Some cars give endless niggling trouble. The dealer/garage fixes the faults faithfully but is reluctant to replace the car with a new one. At the same time owners feel they've been through the wringer and want out of the mess.
That is where it is vital to have bought it through a properly registered garage or a reputable private source.
At least you have some point of referral should trouble arise. But even then some cases can be tricky.

**Your rights**

Essentially anything you buy from a retailer must be fit for its normal purpose, and reasonably durable.

It doesn't matter where this description is outlined. It can be part of the advertising, wrapping, or on a label. It can also be something said to you by the salesperson. Simply put, when you buy a car, you enter into a contract with that person or business. Special deals or offers, or sales, do not remove your statutory rights. You pay a certain price and they agree to provide you with a car.

**What's a warranty?**
**What's a guarantee?**

From 2002, all manufacturers carry a two-year warranty on new cars, on foot of EU legislation. Japanese and Far Eastern manufacturers carry a three-year-warranty.

A warranty is basically a statement by the seller that the car meets certain standards or is as they say it is. In broad terms, a guarantee means the same thing. But there are distinctions.

A warranty also involves a number of commitments - that the car is supported by other services such as roadside assistance, a courtesy car during warranty repairs etc.

A guarantee, under the EU directive on Consumer Guarantees, means:

*The Right to reject faulty goods or have them replaced (this must be exercised within one month of the defect being detected).

*A right to a free repair or compensation for defects appearing within two years of delivery. This is why car manufacturers have moved to two-year warranties.

*And finally the right to presume that defects appearing within six months of purchase were present when the car was delivered. *(This may be challenged).*

Do please check the details as they may vary.

Check to see if it covers parts only, or parts and labour. Many marques nowadays also offer lengthy anti-rust perforation warranties. You need to be very clear on what these mean. If you prang your car and the area around the damage subsequently starts to rust, the warranty is negated.

**First call**

If your car turns out to have faults or starts to give trouble, go immediately to the person or company from whom you bought it. Sometimes distributors are brought into a dispute at a later stage to help resolve the issue at a higher level.

**Refund, repair**

Under law you are entitled to a refund, a replacement or a repair. But you have no rights under the Act if, after even a day or two, you decide you don't like the car and want a refund or an exchange.

You also have no rights if faults were obvious or were pointed out at the time of purchase.

For example, the second-hand car salesman may say the engine 'isn't the best' or the paint is a bit scratched along the rear.

In such situations, you have little grounds for a complaint or recompense. That is why you should check everything out thoroughly before you buy secondhand.

If a car is being sold 'as seen' you are being told you buy at your own risk. Technically, potential flaws have been pointed out to you. Second-hand cars must be of saleable/marketable quality but the level of accountability is lower.

And if you buy something through a private sale, your rights are greatly diminished.

In such circumstances, goods do not have to be of saleable or marketable quality. So be extra careful when buying privately. You have a skimpy safety net.

Remember: a used car being sold privately only has to be owned by the seller and fit their description of it.

**The bad cars**

Every now and then a 'bad' new car slips through the quality checks at the manufacturing plant and a fault is then exposed to the energies and tensions exerted on a vehicle. The shortcomings emerge quickly.

So many elements of a car are inter-connected that the effects of a small problem can spread.

Under warranty, the dealership can repair the faults as they arise. Then something else crops up and that's repaired. Then something else. On it goes.

Seemingly unrelated faults keep arising.

The owner is entitled to feel hard done by, yet the dealership has dutifully abided by the contract of after-sale.

At that stage matters may need to be resolved by a third party – the distributors, or the Society of the Irish Motor Industry which is the trade organisation for the industry.

Otherwise legal action may begin. It can be a difficult scenario and one not easily resolved. There comes a stage when you may have to get an engineer to carry out a thorough examination and compile a comprehensive report on the car.

It can form the basis of your case with the dealer/distributor and/or subsequently your legal proceedings.

**Immediate action**

In general, problems are more sporadic, less serious and dealt with more quickly.

But if a problem arises, do not let it drag on.

Get to the seller immediately. The longer it goes on, the more likely you are to be viewed as partly responsible through your neglect of the problem.

When you make your complaint, let them know in a polite, firm manner that you know your rights.

**Complain**

You should not be intimidated by going into a dealership/garage and making a complaint. You have spent your money on their product.

**Their problem**

If the car won't start, or if you are afraid it represents a safety risk, you are entitled to ask the garage to have it inspected where it is, or to have it towed in for examination. Make it clear you do not expect to be liable for towing charges.

You could also call in a mechanic, the AA or RAC, if you are a member of either, and let them advise you on what the problem is likely to be and the best course of action to take.

You should keep a written note of any difficulties that arise with the car.

A lot of the more progressive dealers now have a customer services desk and that is the best place to start with any complaint.

**Straight talking**

As soon as you get speaking to a senior staff member, keep it simple. Just give the outline of the trouble.

A good operator will offer to take in the vehicle at once to have it examined and provide you with a temporary replacement.

**Note the trouble**

If, for some reason, the seller does not offer to look into it with the urgency you'd like, or puts you off for what you consider to be too long, you may need to issue your complaint in writing.

You should, if you can, enclose photocopies of all relevant documentation such as receipts, contract of sale etc.

Do not include originals of any documentation.

Address the letter to the correct person. Letters can get lost for days in the wrong in-tray. Keep a copy of the letter and any you get in return.

**Legal avenue**

Under a Hire Purchase agreement the owner (finance house) is 'jointly and severally' liable for the goods. So, if matters deteriorate, you can sue them or the dealer, or both.
If the situation gets worse, get that engineer's report to support your case.
Don't be afraid to get advice from a solicitor. If something has pushed you to even consider doing so, it must be serious and probably warrants expert opinion.
Try to find out in advance what that advice will cost and the charge for sending a solicitor's letter.
It may subsequently be a matter of balancing the cost of proceeding with further action against the perceived loss incurred on the car.
It can be a difficult decision and one not to be taken lightly. Get your solicitor to outline of the pros and cons of going to court.
A solicitor's letter can have an energising effect on the other side. But it can also harden attitudes.

**Services**

Consumer protection legislation also covers services.
Here the value of a reputable dealership or garage shines through.
They do the job properly, use the correct materials and get your car back in a safe, satisfactory condition.
Bad workmanship will have to be undone as well as the underlying problems being rectified – effectively a double cost.

**Remember!** There is a lot of consumer protection at your disposal. Don't be afraid to ask the Office of the Director of Consumer Affairs, or the Consumers Association of Ireland for guidance (*See Appendix*).

Chapter 20

# Making the Test work for You

This outlines a series of checks you can carry out on a secondhand car. It is based on the criteria every car must meet to pass the National Car Test. So in effect the test is working for you. It is a useful way to assess, in whole or in part, the state of a car you are thinking of buying, your own vehicle or one due for test.

**National Car Test**

The first test at an NCT centre costs €48.40* and there is a re-test fee of €27.20 if NCT equipment is used to check on repairs discovered by the first check. There is no test fee if only a visual check is warranted. (*As of October 2002*)

The rules are clear: All cars over four years of age must be tested every two years. The system is operated in such a way that you should be notified by post around six to eight weeks before the anniversary date of the car's first registration.

Normally, you are offered a provisional appointment for the test. You can confirm or rearrange a date calling the NCTS LoCall booking number. If you do not hear from NCTS and think your car may be eligible for the NCT, then phone 1890 412 413. Owners of cars off the road or not taxed for over 3 months will not be notified. It is up to the owner to contact NCTS directly themselves. There are 43 NCT Centres.

When it comes to having your car tested you will be notified and informed about the one nearest to you. However, you can have it tested at some other centre so long as you inform them. There is a customer complaints and appeals process should you feel you have a grievance.

**Finding the devil in the detail**

Here, we're going to turn the test on its head and let it work for you, whether you are buying, selling or holding onto your car.
**1.** Firstly, you can use its checklist as your checklist to carry out a comprehensive test on any car you're thinking of buying - without involving a mechanical expert.

**2.** Secondly, you can use it to assess the state of your own vehicle with a view to testing it, keeping it or selling it before buying a newer model.

Using it this way makes it a comprehensive free step-by-step guide. You may find some or all useful at some stage. The run-through is also useful in that it puts everyday language on technical terms.

**Before you start, remember!** *Be careful around moving parts and with other people's property.*

**Your check-up hit list covers:**

Engine/Exhaust
Wheels and Tyres
Lights
Brakes
Steering and Suspension
Chassis and Underbody
Electrical systems
Glass and Mirrors
Transmission
Interior
Fuel system
Miscellaneous items

**\*Engine/exhaust**

Average annual mileage in Ireland is 12,000 to 15,000 but there are massive variations.
Try to focus on cars with 35,000 to 55,000 genuine miles up. Mileage is not the critical consideration it once was. Modern engines are far superior and long lasting. But it still has a major bearing on the likely road life of many parts. A few simple steps will provide a lot of information about the engine.

**Oil be there**

Check the dipstick for oil level. If it's low, suspect neglect and future problems. If there's plenty of oil but it's black and dirty, a service is badly needed. A greyish/white sludge on the inside of the oil filler cap means potentially expensive repairs: the head gasket is probably blown. If you see continuous blue, smelly smoke coming out of the exhaust after you have asked the seller to start it, leave this behind.

**All revved up**

Get the seller to rev the engine. Hold a newspaper an inch or two from the exhaust. If flecks of oil soak into the paper, the engine is dodgy. A continuous white emission may signal costly repairs: cylinder head gasket trouble. Black exhaust smoke may mean too rich a petrol mixture or a clogged air filter. Why is it so bad?

**Settle down**

Diesels are initially noisier and smokier than petrols – at least in the older models. Give them a minute or two to settle down.
Always check the engine is cold before you start. The oil will not have had a chance to circulate and you can hear serious knocks more clearly.
Be suspicious of one that has been warmed up. It will sound and seem much smoother initially. But play the seller at his/her own game. Leave the engine running while you inspect other areas. When it's good and hot, the oil will be thinner and not as capable of hushing worrisome noises. Any move by the seller to turn it off should rank as suspicious. See how smoothly it runs when idling and how quietly when revved.

Listen for knocking and/or clattering. Lift the bonnet. Is the engine oily and/or shuddering? A good engine is quiet when idling and driving. Walk away from anything making metallic noises under the bonnet - or anywhere else for that matter.
An oil pressure light that fades and reappears and a temperature gauge showing a steep rise mean the engine is banjaxed.

**Exhausted**

With the engine running for a minute or two, can you detect little puffs of smoke coming from underneath the car?
Sometimes the connections along the exhaust - from the engine to the rear - are worn or rusted so fumes escape.
If the car is in a garage, have them run it over the pit or up on a hydraulic ramp. It only takes a minute, is no big deal and helps gauge the seller's willingness to accommodate your inspection. Repairs are expensive. Garages charge high labour costs per hour. This can save you hundreds.
Check to see if the exhaust is rusty/badly fitted at junctions along its length? Is there is a lot of oil on the bottom of the engine? Much rust on the underbody?
Can you better see uneven wear on the tyres?

**Only one life for this Cat**

The catalytic converter, or 'cat', is part of your exhaust system. This device is coated with special metals to turn potentially noxious emissions into harmless exhaust gases. It is placed on the exhaust system near the engine. All new cars must have one. But they are easily damaged and most work to full capacity only when warmed up. The problem is you don't know if they are working properly. If emission levels are above designated parameters for the year and make of car, the vehicle will fail the NCT. It is also likely to be badly tuned.

Well worth having an emissions test on a car you're thinking of buying - it's a simple procedure and could save money.

**\* Wheels/tyres**

Wheel rims are often skidded, battered, bent and bumped against footpaths. That spells danger and past misuse, which may reflect, in microcosm, how the entire car was treated.

Fitting costly new tyres to such rims may not solve the problem. They are unlikely to have a sound enough base on which to properly operate.

Also slits, cuts or unevenly worn tyres mean costly replacements and potential danger. Badly worn tyres further suggest previous careless and reckless treatment.

Unevenly worn tyres may mean the car requires wheel alignment. That can be rectified at many garages and tyre centres. But uneven wear could also be due to suspension or chassis problems (See below). Be highly suspicious of wear and tear in the wheel/tyre department.

**\* Lights**

Check the condition of the rear lights/indicators which can be costly to repair, and illegal to have in disrepair.

Switch on all outside lights to see if any are broken or not illuminating properly. If there are several cracks on the lenses, and more than two lights not working, suspect more widespread neglect. Big expense may lurk. The national car test is stringent in this area. Have someone press the brakes to see if the lights are working. And insist you will want the headlights properly aligned as part of any deal you may come to.

**\* Brakes**

With the engine running, push hard on the brake pedal. It should stop some way down and feel firm.

If it continues to soften or yield to pressure all the way to the floor, there are problems.

**Swing to the left**

Often the camber – the slant on the road from the middle to the side – is blamed for a car easing to the left. But its mechanicals should be set up to maintain a straight line under normal driving conditions. If, when driving, you feel any pull to either side, there is likely to be something awry with the wheels or steering. Potentially expensive to put right: at best misaligned wheels, at worst a crash-induced, skewed, chassis. Leave.

The car should also continue in a straight line when the brakes are applied. It should not pull to one side. Even if you are satisfied that brake adjustment will rectify the problem, you have to wonder why a seller would allow a car to be tested for sale in such condition.

**The clutch test**

The clutch pedal should not be stiff or difficult to depress. Many people find this a problem. By the same token, if it yields with barely a touch, it signals problems.
Here is an old, but reliable test for the status of a clutch.
Start by checking the handbrake is working fully and properly.
Park the car in a safe place with plenty of space. Leave the engine running.
Pull the handbrake up to its full extent.
Then, depress the clutch, and put the car in fourth gear. Increase the engine revs a little and slowly let out the clutch pedal.
If the engine starts to struggle/stall, the clutch is in good shape.
Why? Because it is engaging fully and the engine is doing its best to meet the loading being applied.
However, if there is little appreciable difference in the engine's response as you let out the clutch, it is in poor condition.
Why? Because it is not engaging properly there is no loading brought to bear on the engine, so it doesn't struggle/stall.
You most likely face the prospect of a costly clutch replacement in the near future. Leave.

**\*Steering**

With the engine turned on, spin the steering wheel over and back to see how far it goes with minimal force. If there is a knocking noise or an unevenness in its reaction, there may be costly steering linkage or wear defects. *(Never keep a wheel pushed to its extremity with power steering for more than few seconds as it can damage the system.)*

**Bad vibrations**

When test driving, try to take a route that involves a variety of driving conditions – traffic lights, roundabout, main route, backroads etc – so you can better assess the car's characteristics. Also, try to find an area where you can safely make a few sharp turns, to the left and right to see how steering, wheels, brakes and clutch behave. There should not be any clunking sounds.
At 45mph to 55mph, watch out for a noticeable increase in vibration coming through the steering wheel. If it 'jumps' a little in your hands, the wheels may need balancing. Or there may be something more seriously wrong. Exit.

**TIP!** Be wary of bland excuses about anything mechanical. If you notice something you sense is not right, leave it. Someone, somewhere has not taken proper care of it and you will most likely pay dearly if you buy.

### *Suspension

You can make a reasonable, if rudimentary, assessment of the state of the suspension by giving a quick downward push to the four corners of the car – just over the wheels.

This basically checks the response of the shock absorbers. If the car bounces back up quickly and settles after a couple of ups and downs, the shocks are likely to be in reasonable condition. If they yo-yo more often than that, you have problems.

While a poor suspension makes the difference between a rattling, jarring drive and a smooth one, it can also put you in danger if you have to swerve or stop suddenly to avoid an accident.

Once a car is not 'sitting' properly on the road, the loads/pressures on the wheels and tyres can vary enormously. It is like pulling something across a hill; one side of a tyre is doing far more work than the other. But you only have half a tyre working for you.

A good suspension permits greater control: the car will respond better to counteract the pressures, pulls and pushes of a sudden swerve in an emergency. A spun-out suspension will not be able to prevent dipping and swaying. And that leaves the driver in less control and greater danger.

### *Windscreen/windows

Check over the windscreen for scratches and cracks.

See how easily the windows wind up or, if electric, how snugly they fit when fully open or closed. Electric windows can give problems in used cars. So can loose manual winders, switches and floppy sun visors.

Check the mirrors – both interior and exterior - for small cracks. See how well they are anchored to the car's body. Are they original, or have they been repaired or subsequently fitted?

Are there any signs of the door surface being punctured where a wing mirror was knocked off and replaced? Are there signs of rust around them? While you're in that area check the wipers. Do they streak the screen? Are they worn, frayed or ineffective?

### *Transmission

Here you can carry out two checks without employing technical expertise.

Firstly, is there a noticeable whine from the gearbox area when you are in a) low gears? b) travelling at higher speeds?
c) changing down gears to markedly lower speed?
If there is, the gearbox may be excessively worn or damaged. Listen for a whine and if you deem it intrusive, do not buy.
Secondly, if you find changing gears difficult, or if it appears you have to push hard to get into gears you may have gearbox or clutch problems. Not worth the bother involved. Just remember, however, that it may take you a little while to get used to changing gears etc in a strange car.

**\*Fuel system**

Is there a smell of petrol or diesel from inside the car?
Are they any signs of fuel leaks on, or under, the engine?
Does the fuel cap fit perfectly?
Is it the original?
The fuel system is such a potentially lethal area, the detailed checks of pipes, connections etc under the bonnet should be left to an expert.

<u>**TIP!**</u> You can learn a lot by looking a little longer and more critically at what appear to be everyday, straightforward items so you can form a judgment on how well or badly a car has been treated.

**\*Interior**

You can devote as much time to this as you want to. As outlined first time round (Chapter 10), this is the key indicator of use and wear. Heavily worn carpets or seats seriously affect the value of a car. If it has seat covers, lift them off to see what they're covering up. Check that all the doors close properly and line up with the car body. Scratched load areas on estates and hatches could mean a lot of heavy loads.

Take your time giving the interior a thorough check.

Chapter 21

# The ABC of car brochures

Here are some of the more common technical terms you'll come across in new-car brochures and an explanation of what they do to make your driving easier, safer and more comfortable.

**ABS** — Anti-lock brake system. Prevents the wheels from locking under severe braking. A computer releases and re-applies the brakes in milliseconds so they do not lock. This allows the driver to retain steering control while braking hard.

**ACC** — Active Cruise Control, also Distance Control. You pre-set a required speed and distance to be maintained between your vehicle and the one in front. The system maintains both. It will slow down/speed-up the car to maintain distance but will travel at pre-set speed where possible. System applies brakes if gap closes suddenly. There are several varieties of this.

**Active head restraints** — Designed to avert whiplash, especially if your car is hit from behind. The pressure/force exerted by your back and upper body into the seat pushes on connections to the headrest. These lever the headrest forward to support your neck and head. In doing so they prevent both from jerking back at different speeds and so help avert the main cause of whiplash.

**ASC+T** — Anti Slip Control plus Traction. It measures the speed of the four wheels and applies a brake to the one it detects to be slipping. It also reduces engine power and can shut down one or two cylinders. A more sophisticated Dynamic Stability Control also measures how much a car is leaning, for example, and intervenes accordingly. A BMW system.

**ASR** — Anti-Slip Regulator system. It regulates how much power is fed to the driving wheels to prevent skid and slip.

**Automatic sound leveliser** — Measures level of noise in cabin and discreetly increases audio system volume if it deems it necessary (i.e. as car goes faster).

**Bhp/KW** — The brake horsepower of the car. An indication of the engine's ability to generate power and speed. One metric horsepower is the force needed to lift 75kg one metre in one second.

| | |
|---|---|
| **Brake Assist** | - Measures the speed and force with which the brake pedal is pressed. If it determines the driver is attempting an emergency stop, it applies additional brake pressure so he/she can benefit from full extent of ABS system. |
| **CBC** | - Cornering Brake Control. It figures out which wheels have most grip and applies the brakes to them. |
| **Collapsible steering column** | - By 'collapsing' on impact, it moves away from the driver and reduces risk of upper body injuries. |
| **Commonrail turbodiesel** | - Fuel is kept 'on tap' under enormous pressure in a pipe that feeds the cylinders (that's why it's called commonrail). This means there is a constant source of high pressure fuel available to all the injectors all the time. Because of such constant high pressure, the diesel burns more fully and smoothly in the cylinder. This has revolutionised diesel cars. |
| **Cruise control** | - Allows you to set a speed that the car's management system will maintain until you intervene by braking, accelerating or adjusting. Ideal for long motorway journeys - abroad. |
| **Crumple zones** | - Body frame, especially at front, is designed to yield progressively as it absorbs and spreads as much of the collision impact away from cabin and occupants. |
| **d, SDi** | - d = diesel, Common Rail in BMW's. SDi = standard direct injection diesel. No turbo chargers used. |
| **Decoupling brake pedal** | - The pedal is designed to collapse at the moment of impact to reduce risk of leg injury or foot injury. |
| **Direct injection** | - Fuel is squirted straight into the cylinder for burning with air. |
| **EBD** | - Electronic Brake Force Distribution. A computer determines the amount of brake power given to each wheel for a) best stopping control and b) to prevent the wheels locking up. It improves vehicle stability during braking in conditions that fall short of triggering ABS. Helps minimise stopping distance. |
| **Electric power steering** | - Uses an independent electric motor instead of hydraulic system driven by engine. Light, responsive and more fuel efficient. It is speed sensitive - light when parking and gradually increasing 'heaviness' as speed increases so you get a good steering feedback. |
| **ESP** | - Electronic Stability Programme. It brakes individual wheels as required and overrides the engine management system to give more stability in dangerous driving conditions. |
| **Full-time 4WD** | - All four wheels are driven (through a central device called a differential) at all times on or off-road. |
| **HDC** | - Hill Descent Control: prevents the vehicle (a 4x4) from 'running away' down steep/slippery slopes by applying the brakes. |

| | |
|---|---|
| **Hybrid** | - At least two sources of power drive the car. Most common combination is petrol and electricity. On-board computer decides when to switch from one power source to the other. Batteries are constantly charged. |
| **Indirect injection** | - The fuel is fed into a small area where it is mixed with air before being fed into the cylinder for burning. |
| **ISOFIX childseat attachment point(s)** | - Means you can fit a child seat to secure points built into car rather than added, therefore anchoring seat more securely. |
| **JTS** | - Jet Thrust Stoichiometric - a new direct injection system used by Alfa Romeo in petrol engines. |
| **Keyless entry** | - Cars can be locked/unlocked by pressing buttons on the car key. |
| **Lambda** | - These are sensors placed in the exhaust system to detect oxygen in the exhaust gases allow the engine control unit to determine the optimum amount of fuel used. It makes fine adjustments to timing/fuel/air mix. |
| **McPherson** | - Commonly used platform for a car's suspension system. Manufacturers use different variations. |
| **Multi-link suspension** | - Controls the geometry of the road wheels to keep best contact between tyre and road surface. |
| **Multipoint injection** | - Each cylinder has its own injector. |
| **NVH** | - Abbreviation for Noise, Vibration and Harshness. Usually used when carmakers claim smoother engines and greater quietness in a car's interior due to noise dampening materials or more extensive use of rubber mountings for some components. |
| **PDC** | - Parking Distance Control: gives an audible warning of obstacles close at hand (especially the car in front/behind when parking). |
| **Pollen filters** | - protects passengers from dust/exhaust particles and pollen. |
| **quattro** | - A term for all-wheel-drive in Audis. |
| **Seat belt pre-tensioners** | - Rewinds the seatbelts in an impact to hold passengers firmly in place. Means your body is restrained earlier and the risk of injury from being thrown about is reduced. |
| **Side impact beams/protection** | - Steel beams inside the doors designed to protect in an impact from the side. |
| **Supplemental Restraint System (SRS)** | Airbag(s). |
| **TD, Tdi, TiD, dTi, dTC, Cdi, HDi, JTD, CDT, D4D** | - Some of the many abbreviations used by companies to denote vehicles with turbodiesel engines, many with commonrail technology. |

| | |
|---|---|
| **Torque** | - The 'turning power' of an engine. Torque is the power required, for example, to turn a screwdriver or tighten a nut. A car with high torque values requires fewer gear changes and is more flexible and responsive to changes in speed and load. |
| **Traction control** | - Keeps the wheels from losing grip by easing back the power to the engine and/or applies the brakes to a spinning wheel momentarily. By doing so it prevents waste of power and gives traction to the wheel(s) that have grip. |
| **Turbocharger diesel/petrol** | - Uses power, flow of exhaust gases to turn a small turbine. This is linked to a small compressor which greatly increases the air pressure on its way to the combustion chamber. A computer controlled amount of fuel is injected into this. Because it burns more efficiently there is more power produced by the engine. |
| **V6, V8** | - Conventional engines usually have four cylinders in a row - these are in-line engines. Larger engines can be either in-line or in rows of three, four, five or six opposite each other in the shape of a V. Hence V6, V8 etc. |
| **VDC** | - Vehicle Dynamic Control. Uses brake and throttle cutback on individual wheels to keep the car within its grip limits. |
| **VTEC, iVTEC** | - Uses valves to save fuel by using a 'leaner' mixture (more air less fuel) when the engine does not need it and providing it in abundance when it does. A Honda system. |
| **VVT-i** | - Variable Valve Technology intelligent: Hi-tech engine management system that manipulates the intake of fuel to meet different conditions. It closes or narrows the apertures through which the fuel/air mix is fed into the engine. For example, an engine does not need a rich fuel mixture when idling so this adjusts the ratio of air and petrol accordingly. And it constantly adapts to changing demands. A Toyota system. |
| **xenon/bi-xenon headlights** | Use gas discharge technology to produce a much clearer and brighter light which more evenly illuminates the road ahead. |

## Chapter 22

# Reading between the lines - the ads shorthand

Ads can be costly and, in most cases, every word must be paid for. So cars are often advertised in 'shorthand' or code.
These can be baffling if you're buying, or money savers if you're selling.
Here are the most common abbreviations and their explanations:

| | |
|---|---|
| **A/B =** | Airbag |
| **A/C =** | Air conditioning |
| **C/C =** | Climate control or cruise control (*See technical terms Chapter 21*). |
| **C/C cruise control =** | You don't need this but the distributors often have to take it as part of a package. Can add substantially to the cost of the car. |
| **c/l =** | Central locking; a commonplace feature on most cars nowadays. When you lock one door you lock them all. |
| **e/w=** | Electric windows. |
| **s/r =** | Sunroof. |
| **fsh =** | Full service history. A good sign as you have a record of the car's life. |
| **ABS =** | Anti-lock brakes. See Technical Terms explained, Chapter 21. |
| **a/w =** | Alloy wheels. |
| **a/t or A/T =** | Automatic transmission. |
| **p/s=** | Power steering. At this stage it is standard on all but the smallest cars. Older, smaller cars may not have it. |
| **awd =** | All-wheel-drive. Most cars channel their power through either the front or rear two wheels but not all four. Larger cars, particularly executive models, favour power through the rear wheels. But some vehicles have either four-wheel drive (see Chapter 21) or all-wheel-drive which distributes power proportionately to all four. |
| **4wd or FWD =** | Four-wheel-drive. See Chapter 21. |
| **GL, GLX, SL, SLX =** | These denote different levels of specification, equipment and comfort levels generally. Manufacturers and distributors frequently change specification levels to keep pace with the competition. |
| **o.n.o =** | 'Or nearest offer'. Take it as meaning the seller is willing to negotiate. |
| **5sp =** | Five-speed gearbox (five forward gears). Merely mentioning this suggests the seller may be struggling to outline credentials of any |

| | |
|---|---|
| | calibre for the car. 4sp (four-speed, four forward gears) is prehistoric unless it is combined with an automatic transmission. |
| lthr = | Leather upholstery or seating. |
| H/b = | Hatchback. Well-known shape predominates in superminis (see Chapter 12) but appears through most sectors. Usually accompanied by either '3dr' or '5dr'. |
| Met = | Metallic paint. |
| New model/new shape= | Beware. The car as advertised may bear the shape of the new range but may be two or three revisions old. Check. It may not even belong to the new generation at all. Description may be ignorance on the seller's behalf or a means of duping you, but do not take it for granted. |
| Ph kit = | Phone kit, an increasingly common inclusion on mid size cars. |
| Pmo = | Perfect mechanical order. |
| P/A/B = | Passenger airbag |
| r/h/r= | Rear headrests. |
| S/A/B = | Side airbags |
| Est = | Estate bodystyle. Check whether it has been used by, or on behalf of, a company or was a family car. |
| SWBs= | Short wheelbase (on 4x4s) |
| LWB= | Long wheel base (on 4x4s) |
| 6xCD = | Six disc compact disc autochanger. Can be in cabin or boot. |
| Single CD= | Many small cars nowadays have single CD slots on the dash as part of the audio system. |

# Appendix

**Paper work explained**

The paperwork involved in buying a car new or used can be confusing. But it is important to know about it.

**What you have to do after buying a new car**

All new cars, and those brought in here, are subject to Vehicle Registration Tax (VRT). They have to be registered with the Revenue Commissioners. You cannot get road tax unless you produce a Vehicle Registration Certificate for your car.
You can register the car and pay the VRT at your local Vehicle Registration Office (VRO). It calculates the VRT. There may be relief for drivers with certain disabilities.

**Buying from a dealer**

Before they hand the car over to you, they must register the vehicle and pay the tax.
Once registered by the Revenue Commissioners and the VRT is paid, you – or the dealer you bought it from - will receive:
**1.** A receipt for the VRT paid which also shows the registration number of your car.
**2.** A Form RF 100. You use this later when applying for road tax.
**3.** And a Vehicle Registration Certificate in the post within 2-3 days.

Registration plates have to be on your car within three days of the registration date. In reality, they are fitted by the dealer. But if you buy the car privately, you will need to get them. Most motor dealers make them to order.

**Secondhand cars: the paperwork**

If you sell your secondhand vehicle or trade it in, you have to register the change of ownership. This is done in one of two ways depending on whether the car was first registered before or after January 1st 1993.
**1.** If your car was registered before January 1st 1993, you can register a change of ownership at your local Motor Taxation Office.
**2.** If it was first registered after this date, you have to register the change of ownership directly with the Vehicle Registration Unit of the Department of the Environment and Local Government (Address, phone number in Appendix).

## Registered before January 1st 1993

**Selling privately**

If your car was registered before January 1st ,1993 and you sell it privately, you must complete a Change of Ownership form.
It's called RF 200. You can get it from your local Motor Taxation Office.
Complete it. Then send it and the car's Log Book to your Motor Taxation Office. That means the change of ownership details will be registered.

**Selling to a dealer**

If you sell your car to a motor dealer (as in a trade-in), you also have to complete an RF 200 form and get it to your local Motor Taxation Office.
But this time you do NOT send the Log Book to the Motor Taxation Office. You give it to the motor dealer when you sell the car to him.

**Buying**

If you buy a car first registered before January 1st 1993, you complete part B of the RF 200 form.
Then you should detach and hold onto part C as this will have to be completed if and when the car is sold next time.
The new details will be registered in the Log Book which will then be returned to the new owner.

## Cars registered from January 1st 1993

**Selling privately**

If you sell your car privately, complete part B of the Vehicle Licensing Certificate and return it to the Vehicle Registration Unit of the Department of the Environment and Local Government.

**What's Part B?**

You would have received this when you bought the car. The new details will be registered and the certificate sent to the new owner.
The Vehicle Registration Certificate - which you also get when you buy a car - should be given to the new owner at time of the sale.

**Selling to a dealer**

If you sell your vehicle to a motor dealer, then you have to complete a form RF 105. The dealer will have one. Return the completed form to the Vehicle

Registration Unit of the Department of the Environment and Local Government.
Give the Vehicle Licensing Certificate and Vehicle Registration Certificates to the dealer.

**Buying privately**

If you privately buy a car first registered after January 1st 1993, then the seller must fill in your details on part B of the Vehicle Licensing Certificate and return it to the Vehicle Registration Unit of the Department of the Environment and Local Government.
The new details will be registered and the amended certificate will be sent to you. The seller will give the Vehicle Registration Certificate to you when you buy the vehicle. There is no charge for registering Change of Ownership details at Motor Taxation Offices or at the Vehicle Registration Unit.

**Where to apply**

Vehicle Registration Unit, Department of the Environment and Local Government,
Shannon,
Co Clare.
Tel: (061) 365000
Fax: (061) 363480
LoCall: 1890 411 412 (calls charged at local rate from anywhere in the country). Contact information for Motor Tax Offices is located under the Local Authorities heading in all public telephone directories.

**On your marques**

These are the main marques selling in Ireland:
Alfa Romeo, Audi, BMW, Chrysler-Jeep, Citroen, Daewoo, Daihatsu, Fiat, Ford, Honda, Hyundai, Isuzu, Jaguar, Kia, Land Rover/Range Rover, Lexus, Mazda, Mercedes, MINI, Mitsubishi, Nissan, Opel, Peugeot, Porsche, Renault, Rover/MG, Saab, Seat, Skoda, Subaru, Suzuki, Toyota, Volkswagen, Volvo.

Main Irish consumer motoring magazines include: Irish Car, Car Buyers Guide, Auto Ireland, Drive!, Autowoman, Motoring Life, Motorshow annual.

Main Irish consumer motoring websites include: www.irishcar.com, www.cbg.ie, www.motornet.ie, www.aaIreland.ie, www.rac.ie

www.simi.ie is the website of the Society of the Irish Motor Industry.

AA(Automobile Association)
23 Suffolk St.,
Dublin 2 (01) 6179999
AA Legal and Technical (Autocheck)
(01) 6179370

Department of the Environment,
Head Office
Custom House
Dublin 1. (01) 8882000
Locall 1890 20 20 21
Fax (01) 8882888
Internet
http:\\www.environ.ie

Consumer Association of Ireland Ltd,.
45 Upper Mount Street,
Dublin 2 (01) 6612466
e-mail:
cai@consumerassociation.ie
web:
www.consumerassociation.ie

RAC Ireland
Newmount House,
22-24 Lower Mount St.
Dublin 2. 01-6760113
Lo Call 1800 483183

Motor Taxation Offices
Co Council/Corporation
Check telephone directory for nearest local office

National Car Testing Service Ltd.,
Lakedrive 3026,
City West Business Campus,
Naas Road, Dublin 24
Customer Enquiries:
1890 20 06 70
Fax 413 5982
e-mail bookings@ncts.ie
web www.ncts.ie

Office of the Director of Consumer Affairs
4 Harcourt Road
Dublin 2
(01) 4025555
Locall 1890 22 02 29

Cork Office
Norwich Union House,
89-90 South Mall,
(021) 4274099

Revenue Commissioners,
Dublin Castle,
Dublin 2 (01) 6475000
web www.revenue.ie
Revenue on Line Service
LoCall 1890 20 11 06

Valuation/classification Issues,
Central Vehicle Office,
Devereux Buildings,
Rosslare Harbour,
Wexford (053) 61200

Vehicle Registration Tax Authorisation,
Vehicle Authorisations,
Government Offices,
Sullivan's Quay,
Cork (021) 4968783

Vehicle Registration Unit,
Department of Environment and Local Government,
Shannon,
Co Clare.

MA&BS Money Advice and Budgeting Service,
Killinarden Enterprise Park,
Tallaght,
Dublin 24
01 4519630

Cork office: Penrose Wharf
Penrose Quay
021 4552080
Check directory for local branch.

Society of the Irish Motor Industry (SIMI)
5 Upper Pembroke Street,
Dublin 2
(01) 6761690 or 6766332
Fax (01) 6619213

Disabled Drivers Association
Liffey Valley Complex
Dublin 22 (01) 6208731

ENFO (Enviornmental Information Service)
17 St. Andrew's Street,
Dublin 2 (01) 8882001
Locall 1890 20 0191
Email info@enfo.ie
Web www.enfo.ie

Irish Insurance Federation
39 Molesworth St.
Dublin 2
(01) 6761820
Fax (01) 6761943

National Safety Council
4 Northbrook,
Ranelagh,
Dublin 6 (01) 496 3422
LoCall 1890 200 844
Fax 496 3306
Email info@nsc.ie
Web www.nsc.ie

Irish League of Credit Unions
33/41 Lower Mount Street
Dublin 2 (01) 6146700

Rate any car on this basis and see how the marks add up. (Suggestion: photocopy these pages and use as a check list for individual cars)

## 1. Visual inspection

**Your verdict**

### CHECK

| | VG | G | F | P |
|---|---|---|---|---|
| overall appearance | ☐ | ☐ | ☐ | ☐ |
| condition of doors (filler, rust etc) | ☐ | ☐ | ☐ | ☐ |
| door sills outside | ☐ | ☐ | ☐ | ☐ |
| door sills inside | ☐ | ☐ | ☐ | ☐ |
| bonnet (rust/dents) | ☐ | ☐ | ☐ | ☐ |
| boot/tailgate (signs of leaks, rust) | ☐ | ☐ | ☐ | ☐ |
| lower panels | ☐ | ☐ | ☐ | ☐ |
| roof/guttering | ☐ | ☐ | ☐ | ☐ |
| wheel arches | ☐ | ☐ | ☐ | ☐ |
| bumpers (front rear) | ☐ | ☐ | ☐ | ☐ |
| lights (lenses, cracks) | ☐ | ☐ | ☐ | ☐ |
| posts and pillars | ☐ | ☐ | ☐ | ☐ |
| re-spray job(s) | ☐ | ☐ | ☐ | ☐ |
| panels (repaired or replaced?) | ☐ | ☐ | ☐ | ☐ |
| exhaust pipe at rear (worn, black?) | ☐ | ☐ | ☐ | ☐ |
| petrol cap/flap condition | ☐ | ☐ | ☐ | ☐ |
| carjack points condition (damaged, rusty etc?) | ☐ | ☐ | ☐ | ☐ |
| towbar? | ☐ | ☐ | ☐ | ☐ |
| rear lights | ☐ | ☐ | ☐ | ☐ |
| tyres | ☐ | ☐ | ☐ | ☐ |
| dust caps | ☐ | ☐ | ☐ | ☐ |
| wheels/rims | ☐ | ☐ | ☐ | ☐ |
| spare wheel | ☐ | ☐ | ☐ | ☐ |
| windscreen (cracks?) | ☐ | ☐ | ☐ | ☐ |
| windscreen rubber | ☐ | ☐ | ☐ | ☐ |
| wipers | ☐ | ☐ | ☐ | ☐ |
| number plates | ☐ | ☐ | ☐ | ☐ |
| wing mirrors | ☐ | ☐ | ☐ | ☐ |

## 2. Interior

| | VG | G | F | P |
|---|---|---|---|---|
| First impression | ☐ | ☐ | ☐ | ☐ |
| condition of seats | ☐ | ☐ | ☐ | ☐ |
| carpet/upholstery | ☐ | ☐ | ☐ | ☐ |
| seat belt, clutch, brake, accelerator pedal rubber wear | ☐ | ☐ | ☐ | ☐ |
| dashboard condition | ☐ | ☐ | ☐ | ☐ |
| ceiling covering | ☐ | ☐ | ☐ | ☐ |
| interior lights | ☐ | ☐ | ☐ | ☐ |
| audio system | ☐ | ☐ | ☐ | ☐ |
| door trim | ☐ | ☐ | ☐ | ☐ |
| door handles (slack or sagging?) | ☐ | ☐ | ☐ | ☐ |
| condition of switches | ☐ | ☐ | ☐ | ☐ |
| gear handle | ☐ | ☐ | ☐ | ☐ |
| window winders | ☐ | ☐ | ☐ | ☐ |
| electric windows | ☐ | ☐ | ☐ | ☐ |
| central locking | ☐ | ☐ | ☐ | ☐ |
| sunroof-windows (manual/electric) | ☐ | ☐ | ☐ | ☐ |
| lights, indicators, headlights, dim | ☐ | ☐ | ☐ | ☐ |
| hazard lights, foglights | ☐ | ☐ | ☐ | ☐ |
| reverse lights | ☐ | ☐ | ☐ | ☐ |

## 3. Under the bonnet

| | VG | G | F | P |
|---|---|---|---|---|
| Appearance of engine area | ☐ | ☐ | ☐ | ☐ |
| underside of bonnet | ☐ | ☐ | ☐ | ☐ |
| battery | ☐ | ☐ | ☐ | ☐ |
| battery tray/retainer | ☐ | ☐ | ☐ | ☐ |
| radiator (signs of damage) | ☐ | ☐ | ☐ | ☐ |
| radiator hoses | ☐ | ☐ | ☐ | ☐ |

(chaffed, worn, cracked) □  exhaust tailpipe □  number plates □
wings (rust, excessive oil) □  boot, bonnet □  colour of car □
condition of engine top and sides (oily, clean?) □  engine sound when idling □  bodystyle, engine □
                                  revved up □  age/registration date □
                                  acceleration □  use of car (private, taxi)? □

## 4. Seen and heard

|  | N/P | S/R | C/C |
|---|---|---|---|
| Starting ease/difficulty | □ | □ | □ |
| warning lights for ignition/oil etc | □ | □ | □ |
| exhaust emission colour on idling (blue, black white etc) | □ | □ | □ |
| on higher revs | □ | □ | □ |
| suspension (bounce test – See Chapter 20) | □ | □ | □ |
| brakes | □ | □ | □ |
| suspension | □ | □ | □ |
| handbrake | □ | □ | □ |
| Windscreen washers and wipers | □ | □ | □ |
| all-round visibility | □ | □ | □ |
| noise/quiet in cabin | □ | □ | □ |
| gearchange | □ | □ | □ |
| air ventilation | □ | □ | □ |
| heating | □ | □ | □ |

*V/G=Very Good, G=Good, F=Fair, P=Poor. N/P=No problem, S/R=Some reservations, C/C=Cause for concern.*

## 7. History

- Is there a service book? □
- Is it complete? □
- Are all repairs, replacements included? □

## 8. Key questions to seller

- Is there anything serious or major wrong with the car?
- Has it ever been crashed while you owned it?
- What was it mostly used for?
- Where was it most often driven to?
- Who drove it most often?
- Are there outstanding finance payments?
- Has it any peculiar things about it such as veering to the left or being hard to start?
- Are there any guarantees or warranties that transfer with its ownership?
- Why are you selling it?

## 5. On the road

| | | | |
|---|---|---|---|
| level of quietness | □ | □ | □ |
| level of vibrations/rattles | □ | □ | □ |
| from doors | □ | □ | □ |
| seats | □ | □ | □ |

## 6. Documentation

|  | Yes | No |
|---|---|---|
| Is the tax up to date? | □ | □ |
| Has it an NCT disc? | □ | □ |
| Are the following as in the documentation: | | |

## Standing Charges per annum €

| Engine Capacity (CC) | up to 1000 | 1001 to 1250 | 1251 to 1500 | 1501 to 1750 | 1751 to 2000 | 2001 to 2500 | 2501 to 3000 | 3001 to 4000 |
|---|---|---|---|---|---|---|---|---|
| a) Car Licence | 130 | 213 | 249 | 353 | 435 | 642 | 817 | 1142 |
| b) Insurance | 1170 | 1421 | 1534 | 1650 | 1905 | 2334 | 2884 | 3219 |
| c) Driving Licence | 3 | 3 | 3 | 3 | 3 | 3 | 3 | 3 |
| d) Depreciation | 1500 | 1750 | 2000 | 2187 | 2375 | 2625 | 3312 | 4000 |
| e) Interest on Capital | 408 | 476 | 544 | 595 | 646 | 714 | 901 | 1088 |
| f) Garage/ Parking | 3276 | 3276 | 3276 | 3276 | 3276 | 3276 | 3276 | 3276 |
| g) AA Subscription | 91 | 91 | 91 | 91 | 91 | 91 | 91 | 91 |
| € | 6578 | 7230 | 7697 | 8155 | 8731 | 9685 | 11284 | 12819 |

## Cost per mile (in cents)

|  | up to 1000 | 1001 to 1250 | 1251 to 1500 | 1501 to 1750 | 1751 to 2000 | 2001 to 2500 | 2501 to 3000 | 3001 to 4000 |
|---|---|---|---|---|---|---|---|---|
| 10,000 | 65.78 | 72.3 | 76.97 | 81.55 | 81.31 | 96.85 | 112.84 | 128.19 |
| 5,000 | 131.56 | 144.6 | 153.94 | 163.1 | 174.62 | 193.7 | 225.68 | 256.38 |
| 15,000 | 43.85 | 48.2 | 51.31 | 54.36 | 58.2 | 64.56 | 75.22 | 85.46 |
| 20,000 | 32.89 | 36.15 | 38.48 | 40.77 | 43.65 | 48.42 | 56.42 | 64.09 |

## Operating cost per mile (in cents)

|  | up to 1000 | 1001 to 1250 | 1251 to 1500 | 1501 to 1750 | 1751 to 2000 | 2001 to 2500 | 2501 to 3000 | 3001 to 4000 |
|---|---|---|---|---|---|---|---|---|
| h) Petrol | 9.604 | 10.868 | 11.811 | 13.766 | 15.296 | 16.521 | 19.666 | 22.944 |
| i) Oil | 0.129 | 0.158 | 0.194 | 0.222 | 0.244 | 0.255 | 0.269 | 0.335 |
| j) Tyres | 1.688 | 2.095 | 2.196 | 3.022 | 3.085 | 3.288 | 5.04 | 7.732 |
| K) Servicing | 1.879 | 2.476 | 2.705 | 3.149 | 3.263 | 3.289 | 3.898 | 4.383 |
| L) Repairs & Replacements | 6.492 | 7.671 | 8.085 | 9.206 | 10.573 | 11.373 | 14.254 | 17.467 |
| cent | 19.792 | 23.269 | 24.991 | 29.365 | 32.461 | 34.726 | 43.127 | 52.861 |

## Total costs per mile (Based on 10,000 miles)

|  | up to 1000 | 1001 to 1250 | 1251 to 1500 | 1501 to 1750 | 1751 to 2000 | 2001 to 2500 | 2501 to 3000 | 3001 to 4000 |
|---|---|---|---|---|---|---|---|---|
| Standing Charges | 65.78 | 72.31 | 76.97 | 81.55 | 87.31 | 96.85 | 112.84 | 128.19 |
| Operating Costs | 19.79 | 23.27 | 24.99 | 29.37 | 32.46 | 34.72 | 43.18 | 52.86 |
| cent | 85.57 | 95.58 | 101.96 | 110.92 | 119.77 | 131.57 | 156.02 | 181.05 |

*91c per litre (Unleaded).
for each cent more, or less, add or substract

|  |  |  |  |  |  |  |  |  |
|---|---|---|---|---|---|---|---|---|
|  | 0.105 | 0.119 | 0.129 | 0.151 | 0.167 | 0.181 | 0.206 | 0.251 |

### Notes

It should be noted that the figures quoted are average only and where necessary members should substitute actual amounts.
For the purpose of this schedule the vehicles have been valued at:
€11,500 - €13,500 - €15,250 - €17,125 - €19,050 - €20,350 - €25,400 - €30,500, respectively
a. Car Licence: GET PRICES
b. Insurance: (Class 1 ) Average rates for Third Party, fire, Theft policies. No allowance is made for no claims discount.
c. Driving Licence: £4 per annum.
d. Depreciation: Based on mileage of 10,000 miles per annum, and assuming an economical life of 80,000 miles or eight years.
e. Interest on Capital; Car value if invested at 4.25 % per annum.
f. Garage/Parking: _50 per week.
g. AA Subscription: SUBSCRIPTION FEE per annum.
h. Petrol: PRICEc per litre UNLEADED ( €PRICEc per gallon)
i. Engine Oil: Allowance is made for variable consumption throughout the car's life and the cost of replacement after oil changes.
j. Tyres: Estimated tyre life 30,000 miles.
k. Servicing: General servicing as recommended by the manufacturers.
l. Repairs and replacements: Estimated on the basis of total cost of repairs, replacements and renovations over eight years or 80.000 miles.